IN THE PRESENCE OF ANOTHER:

A Lyrical Exploration of Psychotherapy

ALEXANDER BADKHEN

Translated from the Russian by
Anna Badkhen

ISBN-13: 9781793121479   US $14.95

Published in the United States by the Uniterra Foundation.
    Contact: uniterra4@gmail.com

Cover: selection from Henri Matisse's *Music*, (1910)
Collection of The Hermitage,
St. Petersburg, Russia

<u>**Early praise for *In the Presence of Another***</u>

I had always hoped that Alexander "Sasha" Badkhen would write a book about his mythic journeys, his internal journey as he studied humanistic, existential, and transpersonal psychology, and his outer journey as he implemented these psychotherapeutic insights into his marvelous training center on the shores of the Baltic Sea. Much to my delight, he has written both accounts in a seamless book that is a joy to read and savour. Sasha's readers will witness the changes he experienced as the Soviet Union became Russia and as Leningrad became St. Petersburg. They will learn about "presence," probably the key element of any type of psychotherapy, and see how Sasha embellished it with poetry, paintings, and prose. Many writers have remarked that psychotherapy is as much of an art as a science, but Sasha has added another dimension: psychotherapy is also the care of a client's soul. In my opinion, Sasha's lucky clients and students -- and their souls -- are in good hands whenever Sasha enters their lives. Read this book and see if you agree with me!

Stanley Krippner, Ph.D. *co-author Personal Mythology*

Dr. Badkhen has written an extraordinary book, reflecting on the deep subtleties of the psychotherapeutic relationship within the context of the dramatic cultural and political changes taking place in the world today. He begins with an account of how he and his colleagues created the International School for Psychotherapy Counseling and Group Leadership in St Petersburg, even as the Soviet system was collapsing in Russia. As someone who played a role in the early days, I am especially gratified to read how their story has unfolded. Sasha goes on to synthesize an astonishing array of insights from philosophers, psychologists, poets, musicians, and writers—including his own discoveries—into a lucid exploration of the lyrical and soulful nature of psychotherapy.

Molly Young Brown, counselor/coach, teacher of psychosynthesis and the Work That Reconnects. Author: *Growing Whole: Self-realization for the Great Turning, and Coming Back to Life: The Updated Guide to the Work That Reconnects*, with Joanna Macy.

Sasha Badkhen's reflections of emerging from Soviet Russia, where individual experience was banished by the ideology of the collective, provide a personal prologue to his fresh and timely practical wisdom about the importance of the two individuals in the psychotherapy dyad. The primacy of relationship over technique, the nature of empathy, the existential realities of both client and therapist, all of these and more he makes philosophically and experientially alive for the reader. Valuable for both seasoned and beginning therapists, this book goes beyond the ideas and information it includes, evoking in the reader direct, immediate experiences that will broaden and deepen both professionally and personally.

David S. Elliott, Ph.D. Clinical Psychologist; Co-author of *Attachment Disturbances in Adults: Treatment for Comprehensive Repair (2016).*

It's no wonder Alexander Badkhen added a biographical section to his thoughts on psychotherapy, for he shows that in this art what gives meaning is the context: experiences, people, ideas, journeys, in the life of the therapist as well as the patient. All these elements make each session the unique event it must be. So, the author speaks, for example, about such diverse subjects as his struggles with the KGB, a Baal Shem Tov story, the flight of geese, the construction of meaning in how we talk with one other, an encounter with Fritjof Capra, watching goldfish freely swimming in a pond, a foreboding dream by his father, his dilemma of whether to leave Russia (and the decision not to), and any others, all beautifully woven into his life and his work.

A brilliant, moving book - one that will accompany you for a long time in your thoughts and in your heart.

Piero Ferrucci, author of *The Power of Kindness* and *Your Inner Will.*

At this stage in my work with therapy clients, I am not looking for new tricks or techniques on how to become a better therapist. Thankfully, In the Presence of Another is not about tricks and techniques. It is about a way of seeing—how we see our clients and ourselves, how we see our relationship to our clients, and how we see what psychotherapy actually is. With personal anecdotes, case examples, theoretical background from many thought leaders in the field of psychology, plus illustrations of his points that draw from literature and the arts, Badkhen lays out an eloquent and yes, lyrical, description of what makes for a truly healing therapeutic relationship. There is much to ponder, appreciate and learn from in these pages, for both beginning and seasoned therapists. In the Presence of Another is an exceptionally brilliant, wise, deep and soulful contribution to the field.

Abby Seixas, MA, MFT, author of *Finding the Deep River Within; A Woman's Guide to Recovering Balance and Meaning in Everyday Life.*

"By some serendipity almost thirty years ago, a small group of searching friends, in what at the time was the Soviet Union, encountered their American colleagues who had set out toward them first, who, despite fears and prejudices, had performed an act of will and journeyed to a world about which they had known very little. And that improbable, "impossible" encounter gave birth to a long-lasting creative collaboration that impacted hundreds, thousands of people." – p. 189

Sasha Badkhen has beautifully and touchingly chronicled his personal journey and the saga of two professional communities—one Russian, one North American and European—who set out in the '90s to collaborate on the founding of a post-graduate training program for an existential/humanistic/spiritual approach to psychotherapy, counseling, and group leadership in Post-Soviet Russia. He has also detailed the philosophical roots and development of this approach in a wide-ranging discussion of the work of many psychologists and philosophers—East and West—and articulated clearly the essential spirit and values of the whole endeavor.

This is a book that has been important to many Russians who are exploring this orientation to psychological and social healing and personal development, and with this translated edition, its deep humanity and wisdom will now be available to the English-speaking world.

Thomas Yeomans, Ph.D., is the founder of the Concord Institute (USA) and has been a trainer in Psychosynthesis, Spiritual Psychology, and Soul Process Work in North America, Europe and Russia for almost 50 years.

Table of Contents

When I See the Rose

for Sasha

I enter a gorgeous labrynth, not outside me, but in me,
yet not in me, more between me and this other,
but not other and not me, more here
in this soft yellow, this velvet petal's touch,
yet not its touch, our touch, together,
ours and not ours—

Is it not here where rose and I gaze
into a moment, a depth,
yet whose depth…
where our skins meet,
and it's called "touch," but whose touch,
whose caress and who caressed,

where the verb I call me
meets the verb I call rose,
both verbs, or one verb?

Gary Whited

Foreword

You are about to read the inspiring story of a young physician in the Soviet Union in the 1980's and his personal journey of discovery of western humanistic, existential and spiritual psychology. Alexander (Sasha) Badkhen also recounts how, with the help of committed American, European, and Russian colleagues, he used those insights to build a successful school of western-style psychology in post-Soviet Russia. In Part One, Sasha narrates his odyssey with both intelligence and wonder, as if opening an unexpected and miraculous gift being given to him by life – a life very different than anything that had preceded it in his experience in the Soviet Union.

In Part Two, Sasha gives the gift back to his colleagues in the West by extracting for us his understanding of the key principles of the psychotherapeutic relationship, based on his practice as a psychotherapist in post-soviet Russia for 35 years.

Sasha uses poetry, literature, music, philosophy and psychology to highlight the essential importance of the *presence* of the therapist and of the therapeutic *relationship* to the healing process. This is an oft-covered topic in psychological literature, but it is rarely presented in such a lyrical, aesthetic, and soulful way. I hope you will be moved, as I was, by his stories, his compassion and his breadth of knowledge as he describes the depth of the *relational* nature of psychotherapy and therefore, the need for self-awareness and insight on the part of the therapist. In fact, Badkhen asserts that need is primary and fundamental, and supersedes any school or techniques of therapy. Sasha reminds us that the therapeutic relationship is a sacred trust and an opportunity for growth for both the therapist and the client.

My involvement in this book is also about relationship and growth -- mine. I started making annual trips to St. Petersburg, Russia, twenty-three years ago to teach at the International School for Psychotherapy

Counseling and Group Leadership. I was welcomed with open arms and the students were hungry for anything I could share about my perspectives on human systems theory. Few people in Russia spoke English in the mid-1990's and it was hard to get a sense of how my material was being received, understood and used. The students were always extremely attentive, fully participating and enjoying the experiential exercises, and wonderfully appreciative at the end of each class. But it was still hard to form a two-way relationship because of the language barrier, even with the most marvelous translator anyone could hope for: Sasha's wife, Marina.

In time, as more students began to understand and speak English, I started getting a fuller picture of the Russian psyche and the depth of the Russian soul. The students at Harmony seemed to be creative thinkers, able to integrate all that they were learning with their already existing understanding of literature, poetry and human nature. When I ask the individuals to introduce themselves at the beginning of my class, I usually ask them what is the most important thing for them about the Harmony Institute. Early on, I was surprised by the emotion and magnitude of this response:

> *"You Americans think that because the Soviet Union has fallen apart, that we are free now. It is impossible to say that it starts like that. It is a process. In the beginning, what is important in order to become free? People have to experience this freedom inside themselves. History has examples where people have had to learn to be free [as] when Moses was leading his people for forty years in the desert. Because in order to gain new values you need time. I don't want us to spend forty years traveling in the desert and just look to the new generations in the future. I want to be learning now."*[1]

It was clear to me that Sasha had been able to build into the curriculum of the School the insights and true meaning of his personal journey which he shares with us in *In the Presence of Another: A Lyrical Exploration of Psychotherapy*.

Over the years, as Sasha Badkhen and Mark Pevsner and the rest of the leadership group wrestled with interpersonal and financial issues

---

[1] Leo Kukharenko, third year student at the International School.

as they worked to build the school, I often served as a sounding board and coach to them. This coaching was based on my experience as an organizational development consultant, and from what I had learned in trying – and failing -- to establish a similar type of school with colleagues in California in the 1970's. Over time, as their school became more and more successful, it became clear to me that this relationship with them was healing some of my past pain from the failure of our vision in the 70's. Ironically, by their including me in their process, I was able to contribute in a small way toward building in Russia what we had been unable to create in California. This is a gift, among many gifts they have given me.

As I developed a deeper relationship with the School, some unconscious hubris on my part evaporated and I shifted from seeing them simply as the recipients of the material we were bringing *from* the West, to seeing them as true peers from whom I could learn ideas and processes to *bring back to* America. I became more and more curious about what they were doing with the material that I and others were bringing and how they were adapting it to a curriculum that was so successful. However, all of the material they were generating was in Russian, so it was difficult to discern the essence of their teachings. Fortunately, I was able to participate in several conferences where Sasha Badkhen, Mark Pevsner and others from the International School presented in English and I began to hear a little of the "voice," the perspective or world view, of their school. Finally, when Sasha published this book in Russian, the opportunity presented itself to honor the reciprocity of our relationship by having it translated and published in America and Europe.

Here then, is Sasha's gift back to those of us in the West, presented with intelligence, sensitivity to the human condition, and wisdom. I hope you will appreciate the present as much as I do.

Mark Horowitz,
Author, *The Dance of We: the Mindful Use of Love and Power in Human Systems*

Introduction

Change lies at the very heart of psychotherapy; one may say that psychotherapy is the discipline of internal change. And the discipline itself is changing. New methods and approaches have been forming within it constantly throughout the almost hundred and fifty years of its existence. The reason for this is not merely the intramural development of psychotherapy as a field, as a craft. Its very cultural context has changed: by the middle of the twentieth century, psychotherapy has transcended the confines of its trade and become part of contemporary culture. Its use is no longer limited to people who are ill. Psychotherapy has become the very thing suggested by the etymology of its name, which has its origins in two Greek roots: *psyché*, which means "soul," and *theraps, therapōn*—"attendant," "caretaker," "caregiver." Therefore, "psychotherapy" is the act of taking care of the soul, and a psychotherapist is the one who attends to the soul.

The famous American psychotherapist Milton Erickson once jokingly described psychotherapy as "Two people sitting in a room talking together, trying to figure out what the hell one of them wants."[2] But his witticism begs the question: whom did he mean by "one of them?" Most likely he meant the client. But what about the psychotherapist? He must "want" something, too, and both of them are included in the psychotherapeutic process. And is it possible for what the psychotherapist "wants" not to influence what takes place within their relationship? This, of course, is a rhetorical question, because the answer is obvious. What is really interesting is *what constitutes* this influence, *how* it occurs, and *what to do* about it. Plenty of wonderful research is dedicated to the subject, and it is not my goal here to analyze or critique it. What I am interested in are the general

---

[2] De Shazer, S. *Journal of Systemic Therapies*, Spring 1994, Volume 13, No. 1, p. 15

aspects, what we can call the basic factors, of a supporting relationship. Some of them may appear external, but I will try to demonstrate them from the inside, from a new standpoint. I will focus not so much on the proof of their influence as much on the aspects of how these aspects of a supportive relationship manifest themselves in daily practice, and on the ways in which they develop in the process of professional training.

As with many practical psychologists and psychotherapists, it is important for me to know my own professional abilities, to be aware of what, for me, is permissible and what is not, and what kind of results I can expect from my actions. I need to understand how I establish that my efforts are effective, and I need to have an idea for what to do when I see that they are ineffective. Of course, it is impossible to answer these questions once and for all. These questions are eternal, and each specialist must keep finding new answers to them over and over—but that does not devalue their meaningfulness. In a therapeutic space, it is necessary to have reference points, and this is something I want to ponder together with my readers. I want to focus on what, in my opinion, is one of the most important aspects of a therapeutic relationship: the *therapeutic presence* in the process of being with the Other. Whichever term they use for it, specialists who belong to the most diverse schools and directions agree that this common factor is the absolute prerequisite for their work, which is why we can call it *trans-methodological.*

"As the patient represents the object, could one expect to obtain even in the summation of his various experiences, a universal human psychology? It would represent only the psychology of a part of humanity, let us say even of the majority, namely those in need of help. The psychology of the helper, of the therapist, would remain and this side of human nature is at least just as important."[3] These words belong to Otto Rank. They were written a long time ago but they have not lost their immediacy to this day. The statement that the psychotherapist's only tool is the psychotherapist himself has been used so many times it has become almost cliché, but it really is true. It is because of the

---

[3] Rank, O., *Truth and Reality*, Norton, 1978, p. 17

therapist's own personality, and through the therapist's own personality, that the therapist engages in a relationship with a client. And this imposes upon psychotherapists and counselors certain pertinent demands: the emotions, conflicts, inclinations, prejudices and fears within a psychotherapist's own life influence the life of the client. It is the responsibility of the therapist to constantly self-observe in order to diminish the indirect influence of the therapist's own problems on the client. Personal therapy, meditation, supervision groups and seminars are all essential conditions of a therapist's life. In this book, I decided to explore the internal processes of a psychotherapist.

In the first part of the book I will describe a journey. Much of this journey I undertook side by side with my colleagues at the Harmony Institute for Psychotherapy and Counseling in St. Petersburg, Russia, of which I am one of the founders. I am very lucky. Over the course of Harmony's 25-year existence, I have met many amazing people: my students, clients, colleagues, people who came to participate in conferences and workshops. If you go to Harmony's website[4], you can learn about our projects, trainings, and conferences, and, most importantly, find out about the people who populate Harmony and alongside whom I have the honor and the good fortune to work.

By beginning this book with the story of an internal process that I underwent at Harmony, I am not striving to create a chronicle of the organization, however dear this organization may be to me. I am describing my journey, my reflections, and the changes I have experienced because of my work. My vision, of course, is very subjective, but I think that the significance of all memoirs lies precisely in their expression of subjectivity. Besides, despite being subjective, this material also reflects something universal—including general trends in the turbulent development of post-Soviet psychotherapy at the end of the 20th and in the beginning of the 21st centuries.

In the second part of the book I explore the phenomenon of *therapeutic presence*—what many authors consider the most important

---

[4] www.inharmony.ru

condition for a therapeutic relationship (Bugental[5], Yeomans[6]). Therapeutic presence is precisely what creates the energy that allows us to liken therapeutic relationships to a magnetic field that includes two people, the client and the therapist.[7] This field makes it possible to access the deep, internal processes that run through each of us. For the sake of narrative convenience, I have identified several basic therapeutic factors, which I have united under the common designation of "facets of presence," and tried to explore them. It seems important to offer for discussion the various aspects of the phenomenon of presence because, from my point of view, it is precisely these aspects that contain the chemistry of a healing interaction. One can view these aspects as secondary therapeutic tools: internal guiding principles that determine how the therapist watches, listens, observes his or her own responses and reactions, from which internal point he or she constructs hypotheses and makes decisions. To me, these issues seem very important because the specialist's internal position is precisely what determines his or her external therapeutic manifestations and directly influences the quality of a therapeutic relationship.

Our perception of the world depends on how we are at any given moment. We change. Our perception of the world also changes. The book you have before you is about change.

---

[5] Bugental, J., *Psychotherapy and Process: The Fundamentals of an Existential-Humanistic Approach*, Mcgraw-Hill College, 1978, p. 58

[6] Yeomans, T., *Presence, Power and the Planet. Occasional Note No. 1.* Concord Institute, 1999, pp.1-2

[7] May, R. *Power and Innocence: A Search for the Sources of Violence*, Norton, 1972

PART ONE

Becoming

> *There, the diminutive garden where we once sat and recited poetry, now covered in snow, seemed diminished, just like any garden revisited after a period of years.*
>
> Orhan Pamuk

The History of the Idea

I tried learning English a few times but always quickly abandoned my efforts. It wasn't about not having the time—rather, it was about not having any real motivation. A language is, first and foremost, a way to communicate. English is the commonly recognized language of international communication—but with whom would I have communicated in English in my country, which was living behind the Iron Curtain? Most of the people in the Soviet Union who were beginning to study English as adults were the people who were planning to emigrate. In school I took French, but I quickly forgot it because I had no way of using it. I had only occasional encounters with foreigners, and these did not encourage me to study a foreign language. Such was the state of affairs until the mid-1980s.

My favorite pastime was my work. At the time I was working at an inpatient-outpatient government-run rehab, where I was practicing psychotherapy. This was the time of nascent group therapy in the Soviet Union. Of course, the term "group therapy" had existed before, but usually it had been used to mean the collective practice of autogenic training, or explanatory group discussions with a doctor. Also, there existed the practice of group hypnosis, but it would be audacious to call that "group therapy." However, back in the 1960s there began to emerge the practice of informal gatherings: after a lecture (for example, after a collective session of autogenic training), people would have a discussion, which usually took the form of a question-and-answer session, and which usually ended with a late-night tea party. Such meetings were dominated by discussions of various issues that were significant to the people who attended them. In a way, one could have called them discussion groups.

By the mid-1980s, due to the staggering rise of alcoholism, there emerged in the USSR a cautious curiosity about the work of Alcoholics Anonymous and their twelve-step program. However, the idea of a God—even *"as we understood Him"*—that the Alcoholics Anonymous accepted as one of their tenets could not coexist with the propaganda of atheism. Or, rather, it was the other way around: the propaganda of atheism could not be reconciled with such an idea. The phrase *"God as we understand Him"* sounds absurd in a society in which God does not exist. Meetings with visiting Alcoholics Anonymous groups from the United States (which, by the way, included psychotherapists and social workers) taught us a lot.

Sometime around 1987 one such group came on tour to the alcohol- and drug-abuse treatment facility attached to the Nevsky Machine Engineering Plant[8]. The facility was part of our inter-district rehab. I was among the people on hand to welcome the group. During the daytime all the patients at the facility typically were at work at the factory. When the group and its tour guide arrived at the facility there was only one patient present. This was a recent arrival, an older man brought in that morning by a police officer who had threatened the man that if he didn't "volunteer" to start treatment then he would be made to do it, by force. This man had already endured the sad experience of two useless years of forced "treatment" at a compulsory labor rehabilitation center (essentially, a prison). He didn't want to do that again, and so ended up in the clinic for alcohol and drug abusers. He also had undergone "voluntary" treatment several times, though such treatment had never had any effect, but still he agreed to do it again; after all, the conditions here were not too bad, it wasn't a prison. All in all, he made the right choice: anyone in his place would have done the same, and most people did.

Anyway, the Alcoholics Anonymous group arrived, the staff invited the guests into a kind of a living room—a large recreation room with a table in the center—and each of us took a seat at the table. The Americans really wanted to meet a Soviet alcoholic, but all of those

---

[8]*Translator's note*: A factory in Leningrad that designed and manufactured industrial equipment.

were at the factory except for this newly arrived gentleman. He was invited to the meeting and agreed to come. At the table he sat between the translator and me. Then a typical AA meeting began: "Hello, I'm Michael. I am an alcoholic." Everyone responds: "Hello Michael. . ." This goes on for some time, the translator is translating, and suddenly this man (unfortunately, I don't remember his name) whispers to me, "These are not alcoholics."

"Why?" I ask.

"I saw on TV that their alcoholics lie in the gutters, jobless, and these—look at them, they're wearing white pants," he replies.

Although he speaks very quietly, almost in a whisper, members of the group become curious, they want to understand what he is saying. The interpreter translates his words and right away everyone becomes animated. The Alcoholics Anonymous immediately wheel around to face him and take turns telling him which one of them has been fired, and how many times; which one of them has been in treatment, and for how long. But what I think made the biggest impression on our patient was when several people said that they had been arrested for being drunk in public, and one—this was the one in the white pants and a blazer—admitted that he had served time in prison for disorderly conduct while intoxicated. At the end of the meeting they gave our patient some souvenir pins, brochures and books about Alcoholics Anonymous in English, and some small keepsakes. And then the group left.

Here's why I bring up this story: for several years, every six months or so, this man would arrive to pick up the packages Alcoholics Anonymous from America would send in his name to the treatment facility address. The packages contained books and brochures about AA, in English. I don't think this man understood English, but that didn't matter. What mattered was that whenever he arrived to pick up the packages he was always sober, and, reminiscing about that single meeting, he would say: "They came especially from across the ocean to help me." This anecdote seems to be a wonderful example of the healing power of a helping alliance, the power that can reach anywhere, even across language and cultural barriers. It has no borders.

At the time I happened to be the organizer of and participant in many meetings between Russian and American Alcoholics Anonymous. Several times after the meetings our participants shared with me their suspicions that "these Americans aren't really alcoholics at all—they are CIA agents." This was not the demented suspiciousness brought on by a psychotic disorder, because these people were not psychotic. The cause for this phenomenon lay elsewhere. It was possible that they were mistrustful of the groomed, successful appearance of American alcoholics, which clashed radically with the personal experience of our patients, and this inconsistency caused among them a kind of unease that demanded a rational explanation. It was also possible that their feelings were a consequence of Soviet propaganda, spy movies, that kind of stuff. But I don't think such explanations suffice. Curiously, the same patients who felt suspicion and mistrust toward foreigners exhibited complete faith in "sewing," "capsules," "coding," torpedoes," and various other methods of magical healing.[9] A possible reason for this was that the people who lived in the Soviet universe had to put their faith in miracles in many different aspects of their lives. Millions of people huddled in communal apartments because it took practically a miracle to obtain a separate apartment of their own[10]. Same with certain medications, hard-to-find items (which included basic staples—for

---

[9] *Translator's note*: "Sewing," "capsules" and "torpedoes" refer to types of injections that (so the patients were told) were programmed to release into their bloodstream, over the course of several months or even years, disulfiram—a synthetic compound that produces, upon reaction with alcohol, extremely unpleasant aftereffects resembling severe hangover. Often doctors injected their patients with placebos. (See: *Post-Soviet Placebos: Epistomology and Authority in Russian Treatments for Alcoholism*, Eugene Raikhel, *Cult Med Psychiatry*, 2010, vol. 34, pp. 132–168.) "Coding" refers to a practice in which patients were told that their brain was programmed to die if they drank even a small amount of alcohol. Such methods were popular among alcohol abusers in the Soviet Union and, later, Russia in the 1980s and '90s.

[10] *Translator's note*: In the Soviet Union all residential properties belonged to the state, and it was up to the authorities to decide which families got to live in single-family apartments and which had to share communal apartments with many other families, often huddling five or six people to a single room and sharing a single toilet and bathroom with as many as two dozen other people.

example, some personal hygiene products), quality clothing and shoes, and many other things. Access to information was also limited and especially thoroughly managed.[11]

In the middle of the 1980s, when Gorbachev came to power, turbulent changes began in the Soviet society. I, for example, even began to read newspapers. At the time it was interesting—it was the beginning of the period of glasnost and perestroika, and newspapers discussed questions and published articles on subjects that, until then, no one would have dared even to mention in public. At the same time, in the mid-80s, the Soviet government launched a farcical and awkward campaign to stem drinking and alcoholism, a campaign that manifested itself just as farcically at rehab facilities. In his speech "about what kind of psychotherapy we need," the new head doctor of our rehab said: "Treating patients who want to be treated—that's something any idiot can do. Our goal is to treat patients who don't want to be treated." During that same meeting, he had a slip of the tongue, and instead of reading out loud his latest decree "on how to treat alcohol abuse among the populace" he called it the decree "on how to abuse the populace with alcohol treatment." That slip, of course, was a reflection of his understanding of what we were supposed to be doing at the rehab. From his standpoint, a specialist was an instrument of social control and suppression, not someone serving in the best interests of a particular individual seeking help.

All this clashed fundamentally with my vision of what I wanted to be doing, so I decided to quit my job at the rehab. It was a difficult

---

[11] There is a connection between not taking responsibility for one's own life and searching for outside enemies: "Not all hearts are pure: there are many enemies around...and one has to be constantly on alert. ... It's not I who is responsible for my life but my enemies: their evil eyes ruin the ideal makeup of my world. ... The habit of thinking this way produces the habit of acting this way: modern Russians are afraid of the evil eye and witchery and are looking for magical means of defense, which they find on websites and in appropriate literature. The explanatory model becomes the basis of behavioral stereotypes. The habit of thinking and acting form actual cultural beliefs." (Veselova, I., Marinicheva, Yu., *"Zhaba tebe v rot"*, *"figa v kormane" i drugie sposoby otvetit' na pokhvalu // Kompleks Cheburashki, ili obshchestvo poslushaniya*, Veselova I., Proppovsky Tsentr, 2012, pp. 51-53)

decision. First of all, I liked the job, I had put a lot into it. Besides, in Soviet times it was unlikely that you could quit your job and then find some other job. But I did not like the attitude of my new boss, and I understood that I simply would not be able to continue to practice psychotherapy under his supervision. All of this was exacerbated by anonymous accusations against me and some of my colleagues that were typically followed by investigations. The investigations would find no violations but they frayed our nerves, took time, made it harder and harder to work.

The main cause for the accusations was the supervision group. Here is a brief history of that group: Beginning in approximately 1981 or 1982, some young Leningrad psychologists and psychotherapists decided to launch something akin to an ongoing Balint group. There were about twenty of us, we were hoping to become experts, but our resources were limited: we sensed our lack of experience, suffered from the lack of access to literature. Contemporary Western literature on psychology was not being translated into Russian at the time, and getting in touch with colleagues from other countries was out of the question. So we used the only resource available: we learned from one another. We would gather first at our apartments, later at the rehab, where I was the head of the medicine department. My friend and colleague Mark Pevzner also worked there, and later many members of our group came to work there as well. Our meetings took place once or twice a month. We would get together after work and stay from around eight till eleven at night, simply discussing cases from our own practice and the few mimeographed copies of articles and books on psychology that circulated among our colleagues, and we would drink tea with cookies.

During these meetings there were a lot of creative arguments, ideas exchanged, plain conversations. These meetings continued until 1985 or 1986. That was when the anonymous denouncement letters began to arrive at various offices: the district healthcare department; the city healthcare department; the district Communist Party committee; the city Communist Party committee, etc. In response, investigators descended upon our rehab endlessly in order to "sort out" the letters, which meant they would question all the employees (around 160 people!) about who was visiting the rehab, what they talked about, and so forth. The investigators were particularly interested in the ethnic makeup of the supervision group. One of its participants, who was working in a different clinic, was summoned by his head doctor who told him that he had been informed that our colleague was attending "the Zionist group led by a certain Baden."

All of this was unpleasant. But for some time afterward we continued to meet. The meetings were open to anyone who wanted to come, and at a certain point a woman whom the district administration had appointed to work at our rehab a short while earlier started attending the gatherings. She would come to every one of the group's meetings, sit down in the corner by the door, open her notebook and write something in it. We would invite her to join us and sit in our circle. "Oh, no, that's all right, I'm quite comfortable here," she'd respond. All of this was preposterous and funny. But the situation was becoming awkward for group members and after some time our meetings at the rehab came to an end.

The spying per se did not surprise me. But while the existence of informers was expected I can't say that I was used to it. It is impossible to get used to it. In the early 1980s one of my patients reported to the KGB that during a group session I had mentioned Freud. The official reaction was limited to the district KGB officials calling the head doctor of the district rehab and asking him to "act accordingly." The head doctor of the district rehab, an intelligent and decent man, summoned me and warned me to "be more careful." My circumstances were complicated not only because from that moment on I could never feel safe. At the time, we had open group sessions every day, and it was absolutely impossible to know during which of the sessions and in which of the groups the snitching had taken place. Besides, I couldn't help but feel that all the other members of all the groups were also in danger: they were the people who trusted us and who did not suspect that there was an informant among them. It was likely that the snitch was ratting on them, too. And I couldn't even discuss with them what had happened. Today this sounds crazy. It sounded crazy back then, too. But at the time such craziness was commonplace.

My experience during those years helped me see one important (in my opinion, the most important) obstacle to psychotherapy in the Soviet Union: a psychotherapist who worked in a government institution (and there existed, at the time, no alternative[12]), who was retained by the government, represented, in his or her relationship with the patient, the interests of the government. This was not merely paradoxical: it called into question the very possibility of building a *therapeutic relationship*. Later I found a confirmation of this understanding in the works of Thomas Szasz.[13]

In the early 1990s, at Tufts University in the United States, I took part in a panel discussion titled "Did Psychotherapy Exist in the Soviet Union?" I did not have a straightforward answer to this question. Psychotherapists existed in the Soviet Union, of course, but psychotherapy as a cultural institution did not. Around that time Daniel Goleman published a book in which he cited the words of the Tibetan teacher Chogyam Trungpa, who had told him in 1974, "Buddhism will come to the West as a psychology."[14] I think in our post-Soviet culture psychotherapy will take on a similar role of an agent of transformation. It has the capacity to become an instrument of social change. The Brazilian educator Paulo Freire saw in psychotherapy a political medium that leads to freedom. In his opinion, by fostering awareness, psychotherapy helps people to identify their own internalized oppression, and in this way, it is an instrument for the personal liberation from the person's own internal slavery.[15]

Growth presupposes a liveliness, a vitality of the system, and in order for such a transformation of consciousness to become possible

---

[12] *Translator's note*: Private enterprise was forbidden in the Soviet Union until 1987.

[13] Szasz T.S. *The Myth of Mental Illness: Foundation of a Theory of Personal Conduct*. N.Y.: Delta Publishing Co. Inc, 1961. P. 62-72

[14] Goleman, D., *Meditative Mind: The Varieties of Meditative Experiences*, Tarcher, 1988, p. xxii

[15] Freire, P., *Pedagogy of the Oppressed*, Bloomsbury Academic, 2000

the lifeless—as Erich Fromm would have put it, necrophilic[16]—Soviet system had to break down. Which was what happened: the oppressive Soviet system, which had devoured its own people by the millions, inevitably collapsed.

---

[16] Fromm, E., *The Heart of Man*, Harper & Row, 1964, p. 44

Education

In order to become a craftsman one must find a mentor. This is also true for psychotherapy. Our Russian mentors at the time could *interest* us in psychotherapy, and for that I am very grateful. They knew a lot *about* psychotherapy, but they could not teach us the therapeutic process because they had never studied it themselves. There had been no one to learn it from. From the early 1930s until the mid-1960s no one taught psychology in the USSR: it was considered a "pseudoscience." The links through which knowledge and experience would have transferred from one generation of experts to the next were destroyed in the 1930s, '40s, and '50s, along with the experts themselves, the bearers of that knowledge and experience.

In 1986, in the name of citizen diplomacy, Carl Rogers, and, later, Virginia Satir, arrived in the Soviet Union. They did group work, read lectures, held demonstration sessions. Thousands of experts in helping professions from different countries had responded to the summons of the citizen diplomacy movement, and most of them were from the United States. Relationships and friendships were initiated. The knowledge of English became crucial to being able to converse freely and develop professionally. Something always had stood in the way of my ability to study the language, until the following incident took place: In 1987 a group of American colleagues were visiting Leningrad and my wife, Marina, and I invited them over. I don't remember how many people crowded into our apartment that day—maybe twenty. But what I do remember clearly was that one of them started telling me about herself. We stood next to each other by the window and I listened to her very emotional story about her childhood. When she fell silent I suddenly realized that I had understood what she'd just told me. Not the individual words, but the meaning of what she was talking about. I was stunned by her story, by her sincerity and her trust, and by the fact that I couldn't understand how it was possible that I had understood the meaning of her account. At that moment, my own internal Iron Curtain, which had separated the English language from me, had been breached. I started to listen to language audiotapes, to read books, but mainly I was in almost constant conversation with American colleagues. By 1988 their visits became somewhat regular. Often one of them would stay with us for a couple of days; sometimes much longer. Most likely it was because I was constantly speaking to them that my English grew better and better.

This was the time of hope and new beginnings. In 1987 the Soviet Union passed a law that allowed private enterprise, and a small group of friends and colleagues and I decided to create our own organization, and called it Harmony.

Harmony was officially registered on July 14, 1988, and by April 1989, with the help of the American social worker Lorna DiMeo, we had launched a two-year program to train psychotherapists and psychologists in psychodynamic therapy. The program was called the Institute for International Psychotherapy Training. I think it was one of the first such programs in the Soviet Union. Lorna invited wonderful experts to be teachers: Don Brand, Ned Cassem, Albert Rabin, Arthur Seagull. All of them were vibrant individuals and exceptional professionals. Arthur Seagull knew an infinite number of jokes and quips that had tremendous didactic potential. Ned Cassem, on the other hand, was an extremely serious man. He was the chief of psychiatry at Massachusetts General Hospital in Boston. He was particularly interested in the subjects of death, loss, grief. Besides, he was a Catholic priest. Don Brand, who was the director of our new program, had a private practice in Boston, taught at Antioch College-New England, and was also a rabbi. He would later move to Israel. The oldest of the four was Albert Rabin; when he came to us he was around 80 years old. But his age had had no effect on the sharpness of his mind. Once, when he was telling a personal anecdote during a seminar, he said (in English, of course, since he didn't know Russian), "and this person," and the translator we had hired translated it into the Russian as, "and this patient." Rabin immediately turned to the translator and corrected him, in English: "I did not say 'patient.' I said 'person.'" He must have discerned in the sound of the Russian phrase a word he had not pronounced. But it was a very important word, because it designated a relationship: a person, not a patient. It's a tiny instance. But what it teaches is that in therapy words are important, as well as what the words stand for, as well as what the therapist must know to listen for.

Another approach that influenced Harmony's development was the training program in Psychosynthesis. Molly Brown, Janet Rainwater, and Carol Hwoschinsky came from the United States to Leningrad to launch the training in the beginning of 1989.

The workshop started at Harmony on September 21, 1989. I really didn't want to attend it. At the time my father was very ill. In the beginning of the summer of 1989 he was diagnosed with cancer. The illness had spread too far, the doctors said he only had a few months left to live. I had moved in with him and took care of him. For me it was a difficult time. There were several points in my life that I can call pivotal. When I was 10 years old my mother died of cancer. At that time, I lived through an enormous loss. I believe that it was then that I learned to commiserate with the pain of others.

In order to leave the house during my father's illness I had to ask my relatives to take over for me, and I did on this day. At Harmony, I was one of the people responsible for organizing seminars taught by foreign experts, which mostly meant setting up chairs and deciding which room to use. Originally I had thought that as soon as I got everything ready and the seminar began I would go home. I hesitated, but then I decided to stay.

I have, in front of me, my notes from that seminar. The entry on the first page is a transcript of my father's dream, which he had told me the day before:

> *This dream is about Victory Day. We are on a train. We are coming back from the war. The train is festooned with flowers. Music, joy, celebration, everyone is happy, everyone's congratulating one another, there is*

a sense of satisfaction—we have won, we are returning with victory! The other people on the train are . . . (and he lists the names of the people who are with him on this train, these are the names of the people who had died recently: famous musicians, composers, actors, his colleagues and friends) and I don't understand why I am among them, they are older than me by seven or eight years. I want to turn on the light.

I understand that this dream is about the approaching death, about the final journey he is about to undertake, the journey for which he is now getting ready. The most terrible for me is that I cannot protect him, that I cannot do anything anymore…

The seminar begins. The participants divide into groups and I end up in Molly Brown's group. Molly asks, "What makes your heart sing?" At that point I start feeling pain in my chest. My father has lung cancer, and it resonates inside of me. I am very sad and mournful, and I feel worried, it is hard for me to talk to other people right now. I want to leave. Then some borders are erased and it is as if I come to life. An hour passes and I stay at the workshop. I feel that I can encounter myself here, encounter the truth of all the bitter and frightening things that are happening in my life, just to feel it, to stop controlling myself, to be myself. For the first time during this day I feel calm. At night I tell my father about the workshop, the exercises we did, and in the morning I go back to Harmony again.

These were three days of intensive self-discovery, self-examination, and mutual assistance. I answered my own questions, words came from somewhere, I made drawings, I encountered the nature within myself. It was captivating. At the workshop we talked a lot about therapeutic relationships, explored them through different exercises.

I first heard of Psychosynthesis in the early 1980s. One of my colleagues had described to me an article about how to use guided imagery and about how to integrate autogenic training with psychosynthesis. I found the openness of Psychosynthesis, its trans-methodology, attractive. Other approaches fought for purity, while Psychosynthesis appeared to be open to various elements of very diverse branches of psychology, elements that could turn out to be valuable and effective. The author of this concept, Roberto Assagioli, never considered psychosynthesis its own separate school of psychotherapy. Moreover, he hoped that psychosynthesis would never become a separate school. He wanted expert practitioners to have the opportunity to use what was valuable in very different schools, to integrate that into their work. On the last page of the notebook I used to track the events of the workshop and my responses to them there is a note that reflects my astonishment: "Psychosynthesis is something people practice throughout their lives, from childhood. Children's fairytales are psychosynthesis, the introduction of a child into a complete world, in which inviolable ties between people, animals, earth, water, fire mean everything. In fairytales the hero has an advantage if he understands the language of animals and befriends them. Then he can achieve what kings cannot."

After completing the workshop, Molly, Janet and Carol invited Mark Pevzner and me out to dinner. At some point Molly called Mark and me aside and asked how we would feel if she were to invite us to the United States the following summer to take part in a Psychosynthesis summer school. Of course, we agreed immediately. When I came home that night, I told my father about that invitation. He was happy and congratulated me. Maybe for him the invitation was a sign that I had achieved something. He loved me very much and was proud of me. What he and I lived through during the last months of his life was his last gift to me. He died a week later, on October 1, 1989.

* * *

In November of 1989 I received the first letter from a Thomas Yeomans, director of the Concord Institute. It was a formal invitation to visit the United States in the summer of 1990 in order to participate in the Psychosynthesis Summer School. It was dated October 20, 1989. That was the beginning of our correspondence, which later grew into a deep friendship and close professional relationship. Tom was the person who took us seriously, who believed in us, the person who for many years now has been supporting Mark and me at Harmony. But at the time, in 1989, it was a letter from a person I did not yet know.

America

My grandmother Esfir (Esther) had seven brothers and sisters. My father told me that she was particularly fond of her older brother Emil. Emil (Emil Cooper) was a gifted musician. In 1924 he left the Soviet Union on a tour of Europe and never returned. He was a conductor, and worked in different European cities, and before the war he went to the United States, and that country became his home. Although Esfir's and Emil's life journeys took them separate ways and they did not see each other for almost forty years, they continued to love each other. This is evident from their letters. My father told me that my grandmother had felt it when Emil died, even before she had received the notice of his death. He died in the fall of 1960 in New York, and she, in early spring of 1961, in Leningrad. In the summer of 1990 I was flying to the distant America, flying to my future friends and colleagues, flying to the Psychosynthesis Summer School. And in a small way (for some reason I was embarrassed to acknowledge this) I was flying to the country of Emil, my grandmother's brother. It was my first journey outside the Soviet Union. I was 37 years old.

Our Aeroflot flight lands in New York on June 16, 1990 at 1:35 p.m. at John F. Kennedy International Airport. Passport control:

"Do you speak English?"

"Yes, a little."

"Did you come to immigrate?"

"No."

"How much cash are you carrying?"

"Three hundred and twenty-eight dollars."

The officer (a woman) smiles. In my opinion, of course, it is a very large sum of money. The officer staples a piece of paper into my passport. Her stapler breaks. She looks at me apologetically and says, "It's always like that."

I recall my own torment through the agency of such devices and express my condolences. We bid farewell.

At customs control they take my documents and ask:

"Are you from Russia?"

"Yes."

"Very well, very well. Go right ahead."

A middle-aged woman holding a sign that reads "Mark, Sasha" is waiting for us. Her name is Helen. We follow her to the parking lot where she has parked her car, on the fourth floor of the airport (for Mark and me the very idea of a parking lot on the fourth floor is absolutely unreal). The car is maroon, amazing, I've never been inside a car like this. It has air conditioning! It's hot in New York. The engine is soundless. We are driving. Helen tells us that she is an art therapist, that her husband has a Russian friend, Ernst Neizvestny.[17] Maybe we've heard of him? We've heard of him. Helen brings us to a New York suburb, a small town called Hastings-on-Hudson, where we will spend two days. Our host's name is Polly. She is a psychologist, has a private practice, and works mostly with children. She is finishing a book. Polly shows Mark and me to our room, and later we join her for a walk around town.

Polly is walking her dog and showing us around. We approach the local school building. In front of the school there is a big fountain. And here I am dumbstruck. Let me tell you about the biggest shock of my first day in America. It was not the arrival itself, not the rooftop parking lots, not the skyscrapers nor the multi-leveled highways, nor the sound of foreign speech—nothing had stunned me as much as this

---

[17] *Translator's note*: Ernst Neizvestny is a Russian-American sculptor who lives in New York. The playwright Arthur Miller has called him "a prophet of the future." Nikita Khrushchev derided his art as "degenerative" and the Soviet government had forced him to emigrate; later, Khrushchev's family commissioned Neizvestny to design Khrushchev's tomb.

fountain. The thing is, in the water of the fountain's pool there were goldfish. A lot of goldfish. In front of a school building. Later I would see such fountains and little ponds in American schoolyards and on university campuses, they have these amazing fish (most likely, carp) that will eat bread straight out of your hands, that aren't afraid of you. Later I would get used to it. But that first time was impressive. It was my introduction to a world where wild animals walk freely through people's backyards, where birds are not afraid of humans and where humans don't chase them and don't catch fish out of fountain pools. If you don't understand what about it stunned me, then let me tell you the story a friend told me after she came back from vacation at a resort in Turkey in the summer of 2006. At that resort, our drunk compatriots caught a peacock, plucked it, roasted it, and ate it. Of course, they were made to pay a fine, etc. But this was at a resort in Turkey, which means these tourists weren't impoverished or starved. In the Soviet Union in the 1990s people were starved. They would have caught the fish and eaten them.

Later we have dinner and Polly drives us to New York to show us the city at night. It's amazing, of course, but I keep thinking of the fish in the fountain.

The next morning Polly instructs us how to travel to New York on our own. She writes directions in my notebook, and they read like poetry:

> *Grand Central Station*
> *Ask for information center*
> *For next train to Hastings-on-Hudson*
> *Upper or Lower level*
> *And track number*
> *Sit on left and face forward.*
> *Hastings*
> *Next stop after Greystone.*
> *Call collect*
> *Just dial "0"*
> *I want to make a collect call to…*
> *Polly*

New York amazed Mark and me. But it amazed us in its own way. We are on 42nd Street. Around us there are people speaking English and German, people in Indian turbans. A caravan of Hare Krishnas is singing and dancing down the street, under police escort. All traffic is stopped to make way for gilded chariots driven by oxen. People are swarming around, handing out nuts to passers-by, and in the sky an airplane is flying an advertisement banner. All of this at once. Skyscrapers. Limousines. Food smells. We are going to the Metropolitan Museum. After the museum, before we depart for Hastings-on-Hudson, I have a business meeting. An acquaintance in Leningrad had asked me to take a book for his relative who had recently emigrated to the United States. The relative and I have agreed to meet outside the museum. He barely slows down to let Mark and me jump into his car—it's illegal to stop here—and we drive off somewhere. I ask the young man how he's doing. He makes a left turn, slows down to let pedestrians pass, and says, "All would be fine if it weren't for these monkeys."

He points to a young black man who is running across the street. And I understand that all is *not* fine. That there is racism here. And it is particularly awkward and monstrous to hear this come from my countryman's lips. Mark and I need to get out of the car. It's time for us to head back to Hastings-on-Hudson, where goldfish swim in the fountain.

That night Polly invites her friends to a dinner she is hosting in our honor. ("The Russians have come!") The next day we bid Polly farewell and continue onward. Our journey takes us to the train station, from which we will take a train to Massachusetts. We need to get off at a stop called Route 128. On the train we meet other Soviet members of our group. Apart from Mark and me there are colleagues from Leningrad, Moscow, and Vilnius. Several people are waiting for us on the platform. The most famous among them is the tall Tom Yeomans; Anne Yeomans, his wife; Prilly Sanville; Michael Gigante. I think there was someone else there, too, I can't recall. Tom Yeomans has a dog on a leash, a golden retriever called Taran. They put us in cars and drive us to Boston. There we have dinner with the American colleagues whom we don't yet know, and after dinner they distribute us among the people who will be our hosts for the next few days. Mark and I end up with Mark Rousseau and he drives us to Cambridge, the home of Harvard University. For a couple of days we will stay in Cambridge, at a halfway house for the mentally ill—halfway between a mental hospital and ordinary, independent life. It's a little bit like a dormitory. Everyone has his or her own room with a kitchenette, and a bathroom with a shower. Everyone takes care of his or her own food, does the shopping, cooks, etc. There is a large common room that has a TV and a bookshelf with books. A psychologist or a social worker who holds individual or group sessions is always on duty at the house. Mark Rousseau is such a psychologist. His care for us is intensely touching. He takes us to our room, opens a kitchen cupboard—and inside there are bread, cookies, crackers; he opens the fridge—and there is milk, butter, eggs. He places a bowl of fruit on the table and says, shyly, "I heard that there are no pineapples in Russia, so I bought you a pineapple."

The next day flies by quickly. We take walks around Harvard, around the streets of Boston. We talk to new friends. We eat sandwiches on the grass in a park. In America you can walk on grass, sit on it, lie on it, you can play sports on it if you're not in anybody's way. (In the Soviet Union it was strictly forbidden to set even one foot on a park lawn.) In the evening Mark Rousseau rents a movie and we watch it together. It's "Dead Poets Society," it had just come out on tape. I understand nothing of what the actors are saying, I use context to guess the meaning of their words. In general, this entire trip for me is an intensive exercise in intuitive linguistics.

The following morning we drive to Vermont where our first training will take place. The trip takes several hours and the whole way we are listening to the amazing singing of Zuleika, an American singer who performs Sufi songs. While we drive I fall completely in love with her voice and those songs. After a few hours we arrive in Putney, VT, home to the Putney School, where our first retreat will take place.

Many years later I would read in a book by Alexander Etkind[18] that in the middle of the nineteenth century John Noyes founded in Putney an experimental utopian society he called the Putney Commune. This commune, which numbered several hundred people, practiced unusual sexual relations, the so-called "complex marriage," at the basis of which lay the practice of constantly changing sexual partners. While we were at Putney in 1990 we observed no sexual experiments. But there was certainly an interest in the erotic, which demonstrated itself, among other things, in the Russian speakers teaching the choicest Russian swearwords to our American colleague Michael Gigante. Michael repeated his new vocabulary loudly, which made him and everyone around him extremely happy.

The retreat begins on the 20th of June. There are around twenty people in the group, Soviet and American participants and leaders. There are several leaders: Anne Yeomans, Prilly Sanville, Michel Gigante and Claire Boskin. The word "retreat" is new to me. It means a withdrawal, a submergence. Everything is arranged so that we can all together submerge into an atmosphere of self-exploration, a deeper acquaintance with ourselves and with others, so we can uncover for one another even a little bit the particularity of our cultures, see our communalities and our differences. There is a lot of meditation, a lot of working with imagery. Everything is based on the exploration and awareness of experience. A psychotherapist has to know himself; he is his only tool. We learn to stay in the present. We learn to listen. We learn to open ourselves to others. We learn to see commonalities and differences. And to "be with that." There are exercises aimed at exploring therapeutic relationships. Discussions. I sit across from a window, and the window frames the mountains. Such beauty! At night the sky is bestrewn with stars and the air fills with fireflies. In Leningrad there are no mountains. Leningrad is a horizontal city. Leningrad has no fireflies. But it does have midnight sun.

The few days at Putney united us, we learned about one another, we became open to the present and submerged into an atmosphere of

---

[18] Etkind A.M., *Tolkovanie Puteshestvii*, Novoe Literaturnoe Obozrenie, 2001, No. XXIX, pp. 60-64

exploration. We were ready for the next step, and our group went to Concord, Massachusetts.

At the time I knew little about Concord; I had only read that it was a small, old town in New England, the cradle of the American Revolution. I also knew that in the 19th century it was home to Ralph Waldo Emerson and Henry David Thoreau, wonderful American transcendentalist philosophers. I had read that Emerson tried to balance the Western ideal of perfection as a comprehensive development of one's capabilities and the Eastern ideal of perfection as a transcendence of the limits of self, a graduation from a personal consciousness to a universal consciousness. He had always insisted that trans-individual, universal human qualities make the key difference within the microcosm of personality. The life and personality of his contemporary, Henry David Thoreau, proves that for the most part it was possible to achieve such balance[19]:

> *Let us settle ourselves, and work and wedge our feet downward through the mud and slush of opinion, and prejudice, and tradition, and delusion, and appearance, that alluvion which covers the globe, through Paris and London, through New York and Boston and Concord, through Church and State, through poetry and philosophy and religion, till we come to a hard bottom and rocks in place, which we can call reality, and say, This is, and no mistake.*[20]

Unlike their contemporaries who adhered to strict science, Emerson and Thoreau were using daily life to try to demonstrate their vision of the world and to look for answers to the questions that mattered to them. Many years before this trip I had read Thoreau's book *Walden, or, Life in the Woods*. It has this mysterious passage:

> *I long ago lost a hound, a bay horse, and a turtle dove, and am still on their trail. Many are the travelers I have spoken concerning them, describing their tracks and what calls they answered to. I have met one or two who had heard the hound, and the tramp of the horse, and even seen the dove*

---

[19] Ye. P. Zykova, *Vostok v tvorchestve amerikanskikh transtzendentalistov*, Vostok-Zapad, Nauka, 1988
[20] Thoreau, H.D., *Walden*, Imperia Press, 2013, p. 71

disappear behind a cloud, and they seemed as anxious to recover them as if they had lost them themselves.[21]

When I was on my way to Concord I secretly hoped that I would meet such people, that I would recover what I had lost. Because a long time ago, I, too… (from my diary):

Conversations. Ken and Steven:

"What kind of a town is Berdichev? Is it somewhere near Kiev?"

"What about Vinnitsa? Can you show them on a map?" Their eyes are close to mine, they are full of tears… They are like brothers.

It is as if I am entering these open eyes and going through.

And it's not I who has come to visit them, it's they who have come to visit me. And it is I who could ask them:

"My father was born in Odessa. Where is it? Please show me Odessa."

Even the English and the Russian languages have become entwined. I never knew that there are so many Russian words in the English language: "pirog," "sputnik," "blini," "borscht," "glasnost" and… "pogrom."

In Claire Boskin's living room, in the very center of the room, there is a black trunk embossed with tin. Her mother remembers that it contained her family's possessions when they fled Russia.

One young man tells a story:

"She would always hold my hand like this, and she'd turn it palm-upward and say"—and in perfect Russian he pronounces the old rhyme to a child's finger play: "Soroka-vorona kashu varila…"

He doesn't understand the words, he has no idea what they mean, but they come out of his mouth in the exact pitch in which he heard them when he was little. He remembers that afterwards his grandma would always kiss the palm of his hand. Like this.

The Psychosynthesis Summer School took place at Concord Academy, a private high school. It is obviously empty in summer and the school rents out the space for various events. More than a hundred people from different countries participated in the summer school. Many of them would become my friends and partners in various

---

[21] *Ibid,* p. 11

projects over many years to come. It was like a conference: many seminars and workshops, demonstration sessions, roundtables. Morning meditation with Anne Yeomans, during which for the first time in my life I found myself walking barefoot on dewy morning grass. The beauty of nature and the beauty of people. Music and songs during breaks. In almost all the photographs I have from the event, people are singing. I also started singing. It had been years since I had last picked up a guitar, but something had unwound inside and I wanted to sing again. We made plans. We organized the Transcultural Network for Global Psychology and Education (TNC)[22], we decided to hold psychosynthesis training in Leningrad, Moscow and Vilnius, and then for everyone to go to Tbilisi and hold an introductory seminar on psychosynthesis there.

---

[22] The Transcultural Network for Psychology and Education (TCN) was founded in June 1990 at the Concord Institute by an international group of educators and psychologists from the United States, Canada, Norway, Russia and Lithuania. The goal of the network was to develop international professional exchange first and foremost between Western and Soviet—and, later, former Soviet—specialists. Between 1990 and 1995 TCN supported in the United States, Europe and the former Soviet Union a number of projects, including personnel training for the International School of Psychotherapy, Counseling and Group Therapy in Russia. In addition to facilitating professional exchanges, TCN's support included buying electronic equipment for training purposes, as well as books, audio and videotapes for the school library; helping prepare the curriculum; and the certification of the school's graduates.

Changes

Although we did not realize it back then, radical changes took place at Harmony during that time. It became part of the international professional community and its circumstances should be considered in this new context.

On September 7, 1990, a group of our Western colleagues arrived in Leningrad.

From the diary:
When Molly Brown stepped off the plane at the Leningrad airport she said, "I must have been a Russian in a previous life, that's how it feels to be here." And I remembered how I felt during the summer school in Concord: as if East and West were synthesizing within me. Or, rather, my East and my West. And then I recalled the words Marina Tsvetaeva[23] wrote to Rainer Maria Rilke[24]: "I will always be a Russian woman in your perception; you in mine—a purely human (divine) phenomenon. This is the difficulty about our too individualistic nationalities: all what is inside us, is called 'Russian' by the Europeans."[25]

The September school of psychosynthesis took place in a Leningrad suburb called Roshchino, at a government resort built to cater to the employees of the state-owned publishing company Lenizdat. I think this was the first large-scale international event organized by Harmony. In a sense, this summer school was a precursor to the annual

---

[23] *Translator's note*: Marina Tsvetaeva, 1982-1941, Russian poet
[24] *Translator's note*: Rainer Maria Rilke, 1875-1926, Bohemian-Austrian poet
[25] Tsvetaeva M., Rilke R.M., *Letters: Summer 1926*, NYRB Classics, 2001, p. 107

international conference we began to hold two years later. More than 70 people from various Soviet cities took part in the summer school. The training was led by Molly Brown, Patricia Norris and Kallon Basquin from the United States, and André Paré from Canada.

From the diary:
New principles. 'The consensus of one:' a society cannot develop faster than its individual members.

'If you have a mentally ill patient and you haven't lost your mind it means you're a bad professional.' Kallon Basquin.

Searching for my place. From the very beginning this corner seemed somehow attractive. Very early on I sat down in two other spots but each time later I moved to this corner. And I could not leave it.

An exercise out of doors. I left the gates of the resort and walked toward the forest. Puddles stood in the road though it had been a long time since it had rained last. I walked on the road. Ducks flew, shrieking, headed south. Around the bend in the road I saw a river. The riverbank completely trashed, some kind of hubcaps, tar, a dead rat by a tree. I felt ill at ease. I returned to the road. I came up to a tree and touched it. Sap stayed on my hands. The word "purification" came to mind. Everything needs to be purified. So do I. I can't seem to be comfortable. Who am I? I am learning myself, discovering myself."

Conferences

*Never doubt that a small group of thoughtful,
committed citizens can change the world; indeed,
it's the only thing that ever has.*

Margaret Mead

The idea to involve Harmony in hosting international conferences finally took shape in 1992, after Mark Pevzner and I attended a conference of the American Association of Humanistic Psychology in the United States. We attended at the invitation of Steve Olweean, whom we had met when he came to Russia in 1990. At the time, groups of American psychologists visited us fairly often, and they frequently participated in gatherings and seminars organized by Harmony and attended by St. Petersburg[26] psychologists and psychotherapists. These visits offered room for professional exchange, providing dozens of Soviet psychologists and psychotherapists the opportunity to openly communicate with their American colleagues, who, in turn, shared with them professional knowledge and experience. These were unique experiences, it is impossible to overestimate the importance of these gatherings.

In May of 1992, at Steve's invitation, Mark and I arrived in the United States. It was my longest visit to America, almost three months.

---

[26] *Translator's note*: St. Petersburg, as the city was originally called, was renamed Petrograd in 1914, Leningrad in 1924. The city's name was changed back to St. Petersburg in 1991.

At first we lived in Kalamazoo, a small university town in the Midwest, in Michigan. Steve enrolled us in training at Gryphon Place, a center for social and psychological help. We spent the first few weeks learning from within the workings of the system of social and psychological help. I must say the system worked great. We tried to absorb the spirit that reigned there and to learn various professional skills, all the while trying to picture how we could apply them at home. Gryphon Place had an excellent training program for hotline volunteers, and we took part in that training as well. Much of what we learned there we later incorporated at Harmony.

We had plenty of time in Kalamazoo to walk, look, dream, read, make plans. During a seminar at the house of one of our American colleagues we met Richard Schwartz, who was then beginning to teach his Internal Family Systems Model, which he had recently developed.

Although my knowledge of English was still very modest, I started reading in English, borrowing books from Steve's vast home library. I came across a copy of Fritjof Capra's *Uncommon Wisdom: Conversations with Remarkable People*[27], at the time only recently published. The book is composed of transcripts of his conversations with prominent scientists. I think it begins with his dialogue with Gregory Bateson. I think there are also conversations with Carl Simonton, R. D. Laing, Krishnamurti, Werner Heisenberg and others whom I no longer recall. But I do remember the two related sensations I felt while I read it: admiration for the freedom and openness with which Capra's interlocutors shared their ideas, and my emergent sense of joy at encountering a world that until then had been closed to me. Of course, the very ideas of Capra's interviewees were astounding, but what impressed me was not so much the content of the conversations as the space for relationships that these conversations created for me: because of the book these people came into dialogue with *me*. It was as if, reading Capra, I myself was present during the conversations with Bateson, Simonton, Laing. These were people about whom I had heard a lot, but I had never thought or dreamed I would meet or talk to them.

---

[27] Capra, F., *Uncommon Knowledge: Conversations with Remarkable People*, Bantam, 1989

And I also felt bitter that for many decades my colleagues and I had been cheated, had no way to converse and exchange ideas freely, had been forced to memorize absurdities and to limit our professional and personal opportunities. As a result, we had also limited the opportunities of those whom we were supposed to be helping.

As part of the visit Steve had planned for us, we participated in the 30th annual conference of the American Association for Humanistic Psychology in San Francisco. Our presentation was titled "From Russia with Love." The title, I admit, was rather bland, and it exploited the name of a famous James Bond film. But the agenda for the event had already been printed: the organizers obviously thought the title attractive. This was my first experience participating in such a large international conference, and it was different from the conferences I had attended in Russia in many respects. Here I was able to meet people about whom, until then, I had only read. These meetings were probably the most important aspect of the conference for me.

During the conferences I had attended in Russia the participants would read reports. And here no one read any reports, and even if there was anything resembling a lecture it was accompanied by a discussion. But the difference wasn't just about form. In the Soviet era, conferences were always organized literally from above, by the state. They were vertical conferences. Here everything was multilayered. There was a huge choice of seminars and workshops. And it was literally a choice, because five or six events took place at once, and all of them seemed very interesting. It was simply impossible to attend all of them. My friends and I took part in different seminars and workshops so that later we could compare notes about what each of us had seen and heard.

I remember that the first event I attended was Bernie Siegel's workshop about working with physically impaired people. Bernie Siegel himself sat in a wheelchair, but not because he couldn't sit in a regular chair. He was perfectly healthy. It was simply that this way he had the opportunity to experience what it was like to be bound to a wheelchair: it was difficult to reach the light switch, it was difficult to open the door to the auditorium. The workshop was dedicated to the psychological exploration of one's physical state. That same day, I went to the lecture of Ashley Montagu, and later to a roundtable with Clark Moustakas… For me these names had been linked to the history of psychology and psychotherapy. My command of the English language didn't allow me to understand everything they were saying—they spoke too fast for me—but I listened and watched, I breathed, I lived together with these people.

On the last day of the conference, a few minutes before the closing ceremony, the newly elected president of the Association, Sandra "Sandy" Friedman, came up to me and said: "I have a request for you. Could you please present Fritjof Capra to the members of the audience? Here he is, let me introduce the two of you." Knowing Sandy—she is a very witty and joyful person—I immediately understood that she was planning some kind of a joke. After she introduced us, Capra told me, "Sasha, I'm glad that you are introducing me, but I have to warn you that everyone in the audience knows who I am."

A minute later I came onstage and said something along these lines:

"I am honored to introduce someone, but since you all know him very well already, instead of telling you about him let me tell you about myself. I came from Russia. This conference for me is an invaluable experience, professionally and personally. I feel this particularly strongly because I have lived my whole life in a country where, until recently, there was no freedom of speech and no freedom of relationships, where it was impossible to imagine the kind of free interaction between people from different cultures that I am seeing here, the kind of interaction in which I am now taking part. It may be difficult for you to imagine this, but because of censorship we were not able to freely read the books on psychology and psychotherapy published in the West. So now I want to introduce to you a person to whom I feel tremendously grateful. A few weeks ago, I read one of his recent books, a book about his encounters with remarkable people—modern philosophers, thinkers, psychologists, doctors. Without him I could never have met them. I know from experience how important it is to have the ability to meet people, to be free and open in relationships, including professional relationships. I am introducing to you a remarkable person whom you, of course, all know very well: Fritjof Capra!"

To be honest, I think this is a much-improved version of what I really said, because my English at the time hardly would have allowed me to make such a speech. But this is exactly what I wanted to say, what I had meant to say.

On our first night back in Kalamazoo after California we didn't go to sleep until late (maybe because we were so overwhelmed by our impressions, or maybe because of the three-hour time difference, or, quite likely, for both of these reasons). We sat in the kitchen, talking, sharing again and again our impressions from the conference. "Why can't we organize a conference like this in Russia?" And almost right away, Steve Olweean suggested that we dedicate it to the subject of conflict resolution. That's how we came up with the title: the International Conference on Conflict Resolution. In the morning we decided it would be an annual conference. Ideas arrived spontaneously. The motto of the conference in San Francisco was "If Not Now, When?" In a way, it remained our motto while we were devising our own conference. In August, right after we returned home to Russia, Harmony began to prepare for its first international conference on conflict resolution.

We didn't have a lot of time to prepare because we had planned to hold the conference in May of 1993. Our conference was devised, first of all, as a space where different people from different countries, people with different opinions and different worldviews, could interact freely. Now we had to actually bring them together. Our idea may have seemed pretty crazy: we had neither experience nor any particular resources, so the enterprise itself was very risky. But we had an enormous desire to go through with it, and we were certain that such an event was necessary and useful. We believed that if we were able to create a space like that, it would become a space where participants could truly interact, exchange experiences, and grow. Only nine months passed from the moment when we came up with this idea to the moment when it became reality.

There were a lot of organizational problems: where to hold the conference, how many translators we would need, how to organize interaction between people who didn't speak the same language. We had to resolve logistical issues, organize visas and registration for international participants, organize lodging, food, communications (we didn't even have a fax machine, not to mention email).

I am now holding in my hands the agenda for that first conference. A letter-size piece of paper bent in half, already yellowed with time: twenty years have passed. Claudio Naranjo, Natalie Rogers and Sandra Friedman sent a videotaped message to all the participants—approximately 350 people from Russia, the United States, Ukraine, Belarus, Kyrgyzstan, Israel and Estonia. The title of one of the presentations today seems touching, "Fax Communication and Its Implications for World Peace"—oh, if only we'd had our own fax machine back then!

Life itself suggested ideas for our conferences: these ideas permeated the atmosphere around us, they were felt in the tension in the air. In the 1990s, after the collapse of the Soviet Union, Russia engaged in internal warfare and we gained significant experience working with victims of conflicts and with veterans. In 2000, we organized a national conference called "War and Trauma." For a few days we managed to bring under the same roof veterans, active-duty troops, practicing therapists and human rights workers. It seemed that until then no one had gathered in close quarters such a toxic mixture of opinions, positions, and worldviews seasoned with a significant dose of mutual paranoia. Of course, all of these opinions existed within the boundless expanses of our country. But the people who espoused them couldn't tolerate one another and preferred not to intersect, and so their views remained unheard—and, therefore, unheeded. This was a kind of social schizophrenia.

In all honesty, I must say that we were quite bewildered when from the very start of the conference the tension and the intolerance among the participants boiled over. One of the participants was so full of wrath, outrage, and, apparently, many other emotions, that she fainted during her own presentation. In the beginning we even worried whether we would be able to direct the process of the conference under such circumstances. And yet the alchemy of the space we had created was such that the participants ended up to hear one another. Many participants later said that the dialogue that took place at that conference was a valuable experience.

That was when we came up with the idea for a conference titled "Self and the Other: the Space for Dialogue," which we continue to hold annually. We have learned to create a space where dissimilar people can come together to be heard and to better understand themselves and others. A human being is not some island in the ocean, people are not solitary in nature, and it is useless to pretend that you can ignore the opinion of someone else if you don't like that opinion. Such fantasies are not simply unhealthy—they are dangerous. Abraham Lincoln once said: "I don't like that man. I must get to know him better." Think about the wisdom of this phrase. Wouldn't it be wonderful if people today thought the same way?

The Choice

Once, I think it was in the fall of 1992, Sergei Sergeyevich Libikh invited me to talk about psychosynthesis during one of his Wednesday gatherings. Professor Libikh is a wonderful lecturer and a very interesting man. For many years he was the dean of psychotherapy and medical psychology at the Leningrad State Institute for the Professional Advancement of Doctors, now known as the St. Petersburg Medical Academy for Postgraduate Education. In the 1970s and 1980s nearly all psychotherapists and clinical psychologists from Leningrad (and other cities) studied under his supervision. For years he would call up his former students once every couple of months and invite them to the upcoming gatherings. "Hello, this is Professor Libikh speaking!" These monthly "Libikh Wednesdays," as we called them, were held at a psychiatric hospital known as the Neurosis Clinic, on Vasilievsky Island. During the Soviet times they represented something extraordinary, a sort of a Noah's ark that would bring together the most diverse Leningrad specialists who were interested in psychotherapy. It was what today we would call a hangout, an informal professional club that survived in the Soviet times from the mid-1970s until the mid-'90s, when Libikh left the clinic.

Given our own sad experience with informal professional gatherings this was quite an unusual affair. The people who presented at the Wednesdays would make a short report (about half an hour long) and then answer questions (for another half an hour). Libikh would moderate, and after this part was over, all the participants would drink tea with the pastries they themselves would bring. As I recall, on the night of my presentation, I shared my ideas about psychosynthesis and told my colleagues about the interesting programs and conferences I had been fortunate enough to attend in the United States and in Norway. I think my colleagues found the ideas of psychosynthesis interesting. But what I remember most clearly from that night is the question a young woman in the audience asked after I spoke about my latest visit to the United States. She asked, "Why did you return, why didn't you stay in America?"

For me, the process of founding Harmony coincided with tormented deliberations over whether I should emigrate. Soon after Harmony was registered with municipal authorities, one of its founders, Roman Gleyzer, announced that he was moving to the United States. He left in 1989 with his parents, who wanted to use their last chance to emigrate. The political situation in the Soviet Union was changing rapidly and it was clear that the rules and norms that had guided Soviet emigration to America were also bound to change before long. During those years, thousands of people crowded outside foreign consulates and embassies to apply for immigration. A torrent of people who wanted to break free poured out of the Soviet Union. This torrent swept away my friends and colleagues. The economic situation in the country was becoming more dire. Everyone in the USSR was used to shortages, but now you couldn't get even the most basic stuff: soap, flour, butter. People stood in enormous lines to buy milk. In 1988, Marina and I had our second daughter, Sonya. In order to buy milk for her either I or our eldest daughter, Anya, had to rush to the dairy shop before it opened in the morning because if we got there any later the milk was likely to have run out. Lines formed in front of stores to buy literally anything these stores would sell. People would stand in lines simply to enter a store, which could end up not selling anything at all. But you could find out that it wasn't selling anything only after you had managed to squeeze inside. Empty counters and aisles bare except for three-liter glass jars of birch juice—that was what a typical grocery store looked like at the time. People would buy absolutely anything. They became irritable, they swore at one another in line, someone would be crying, someone else would be threatening someone and cussing.

But this proved to be less of a deciding factor for me than some far more unpleasant social processes. Parallel to the changes that could have been interpreted as democratization came the escalation of nationalistic attitudes. There were rallies calling for pogroms against Jews, and street corners and entryways to apartment buildings were plastered with hate-mongering leaflets and posters. The media was talking about the resurrection of "Russian fascism." More and more often, Germany on the eve of Nazism came to mind. Even without the media it was enough to read the anti-Semitic slogans on the walls, to listen to the exhortations that carried from the loudspeakers of demonstrators (we lived near Manezhnaya Square, where such rallies often took place). Once, one of our neighbors (usually, when he was drunk, he liked to stand in the courtyard bragging that he was a KGB colonel; I think he now works at the Ministry of Culture in Moscow) asked me why I was not leaving for my "historical Motherland," hinting that it was about time that I did. All of this was not merely sad or frightening, it also begged the question: Did I even have the right to stay in Russia? I had two children and I had to consider their future. Yes, it was true that here, at home, I had my friends and an interesting job, but don't they also need psychotherapists in the West? Why should it matter where I helped people? Was I not leaving because I was afraid of hardship? What was I afraid of more: pogroms at home or professional obstacles in America? I watched a lot of my friends leave, I watched the already uncomfortable way of life crumble, and I did not know what to do. What lay ahead for us here, what kind of future did we have? It was a dumb question that no one could ever answer, but it surfaced often.

All this reminded me of a joke. There's a flood, the water is rising, everyone is trying to run away somewhere, to save themselves, but one Orthodox Jew is just praying and does nothing. Finally someone passes him by and says, "Look, the water is rising, come with us." But he says, "The Almighty will take care of me." Now the water is up to his waist, and once more someone comes to fetch him, to rescue him. But he stubbornly continues to say that there's no need to do anything, that God will take care of him. When the water reaches his throat a boat comes for him, and the people onboard call him to join them. And yet again the Jew turns down their invitation, "I will pray and He will take care of me." Finally the water rises even higher and he drowns. And he appears before God. And he asks God why He had not offered to rescue him. "But I sent for you thrice!" says God.

At last I resolved to leave and obtained an immigration application form for the United States. I made copies of the form (every adult in the family had to fill out his or her own form) and was ready to submit the copies to the American embassy in Moscow. I write, 'I was ready,' but in fact it wasn't that simple. I was tormented from within by the question of whether I should be leaving. Who leaves? Who stays? I thought of my American friends who spoke with gratitude about their grandmothers and grandfathers, fathers and mothers, who had fled Nazi Europe in time. Who shared their recollections of the relatives who did not leave in time and perished. Maybe Marina and I had to become those parents who left, who saved our children and grandchildren by taking them out of a dangerous place? Stop thinking about yourself! Think of the children! Such questioning occurred so frequently that it became a kind of permanent internal backdrop. Like during meditation, when you always come back to your breath, I kept coming back to the same constant thought: Think of the children!

Once—this was in spring, right before Mark's and my trip to the United States in 1992—I was walking through a large courtyard on my way to Harmony. In the center of the courtyard, in a tiny park, a handful of small children were playing on a playground. As I passed them I had a thought that stunned me: Alright, I can leave and in that way take care of *my* children. But then who will take care of *these* children, of *the other* children, who can't leave? What, to leave them to the fascists? Ambushed by my own questions, I at once saw the situation in a different light. No! I don't want this to happen! I don't want to allow this to happen! Let the fascists themselves get out, this is my country. I want to live here, and I will live here. If someone doesn't like that—let them get the hell out! At that moment, I felt so much anger that suddenly I stopped being afraid and having doubts. A kind of certainty, strength, decisiveness and clarity formed inside me.

I stopped feeling like a victim. I think I saw what I needed to do next. Soon afterward I tore up the immigration forms. In this manner I solved my emigration dilemma.

To the question at the Libikh Wednesday—"Why did you return, why didn't you stay in America?"—I responded: "This is where my friends are, my job, what I live for." I did not go into details at the time.

That question, to be fair, returned to me several times since, but the answer was already *inside* of me while the question remained *outside*.

The Concord-Harmony Project

The idea of a joint education project was something Mark Pevzner and I discussed with Tom Yeomans back in 1990, soon after I met him. In March 1991, Tom wrote Harmony a letter that contained a rough draft of a future three-year education course. We formulated its final version in the summer of 1992, when Mark and I came to Concord to attend the summer school for spiritual psychology that Tom ran every year. During that time, in multiple conversations with Tom, the project took final shape. I can even point to the exact spot where that happened—on the lawn in front of Concord Academy, under a big, shady tree. Later we would use the expression "meeting under a tree." The main goal of the project was to create in St. Petersburg a training center that would meet the modern standards for instruction for practicing specialists in therapy and counseling.

Tom founded the Concord Institute in 1990. He was the initiator and the organizer of several Concord summer schools and conferences on psychosynthesis and spiritual psychology. Born in New England, Tom had a brilliant educational background: he studied music and literature at Harvard in the United States and at Oxford in England. In the end of the 1960s-early 1970s, he became interested in psychology and teaching. He got a master's degree from the University of California, where he studied gestalt therapy under George Brown; then a PhD. George and his wife, Judith, are wonderful gestalt therapists who for many years had worked with Fritz Perls. Eventually Judith would visit St. Petersburg three times and would hold trainings for Harmony faculty and our graduates. During his studies under George, Tom met George's other students, among them Nils Grendstad from Norway and Marco de Vries from Holland.

In the United States, and particularly in California, which is open to everything new, original and extravagant, the 1960s and the beginning of the 1970s was the era during which the ideas of humanistic psychology blossomed. New branches of therapy appeared one after another. Psychology in America developed vigorously. It was a time of hope, of creative search and experiments. Around that time Tom became interested in psychosynthesis and together with his wife, Anne, went to Italy to study under Assagioli. Tom recalled that at the time he was a very serious young man, he spent a lot of time reading and thinking while Anne, on the contrary, was more open and attuned to emotional comprehension. After the first meeting and introductions, Assagioli advised Tom to take more walks and delight in nature. Seeing Tom's desire to dig into the essence of things, he would say, "And remember to leave some room for the Mystery." To Anne he gave written assignments, and she had to spend a lot of time with books at the library. After several months, upon returning to California, Tom and Anne began to work at the Psychosynthesis Institute on Sacramento Street in San Francisco. This institute lasted about ten years, and then it disintegrated.

In the early 1980s, Tom and Anne and their sons moved from California to Concord, Massachusetts. Here they immediately felt like outsiders: the cultures of New England and California were very different. Concord was home to the so-called upper middle class, which cultivated a state of calm and wellbeing. Of course, if you were to walk a couple of miles away from Main Street the manicured landscape of Concord would change. Tom liked to walk in the woods around Walden Pond. According to Tom, in the early 1980s these woods were chockfull of garbage. Every day Tom would go there in his oilskin jacket with large pockets, and in the course of his walk he would fill his pockets with empty bottles and cans, which he would later take to the dump. He was possibly the only resident of Concord at the time who cleaned the forest. And he truly cleaned it up! Tom removed thousands of bottles and cans. Once, when he was coming out of the woods with empty bottles in his hands and pockets, he came across two women who were frightened when they saw him: they mistook him for a vagrant.

Clearly, Tom's unconventional behavior did not help the locals to accept him as part of their family. Tom's lifestyle was uncommon among the people who surrounded him: in addition to practicing psychotherapy he wrote poetry, painted, played music. After a couple of years, he published a children's book, with illustrations by a good artist, and this beautifully designed Christmas fairytale appeared in the window of Concord's main bookstore. Tom was asked to read his book to children at the library. Quite a few children came, and they liked the fairytale, and after that the attitude toward Tom changed: now he became a "local author." To be a "local author" in Concord is an honor: among its "local authors" are Thoreau and Emerson. Besides, this status allowed for a few concessions: for example, now Tom could walk anywhere in his denim jeans without attracting unwelcome stares.

One time in the woods Tom found an abandoned or lost dog, brought it home, and named it Taran. During our visits to Concord, Mark and I developed a ritual of walking Taran. Or maybe it was Taran who was walking us. Straining the leash, the dog would run following a road it alone knew, while Mark and I followed it, engrossed in conversation. During one such walk, I think it was in 1993, we came up with a name for the three-year educational program we wanted to create at Harmony. We returned and told Tom that the program we were working on would be called "The International School of Psychotherapy, Counseling, and Group Leadership." Tom approved of the name. He only asked: "Why this particular order, 'psychotherapy, counseling, and group leadership?' Wouldn't it be better to call it the school of counseling, psychotherapy, and group leadership?" I said I didn't know why, except that this was what Mark and I came up with while walking Taran, and for that reason it made sense to leave it as it was. So we did.

The project presupposed that Mark and I would make quarterly visits to the United States to study, participate in the training Tom was leading, visit local educational centers and universities, meet with colleagues. During these visits we underwent clinical supervision with Tom and took part in fundraisers to finance the project.

Between 1993 and 1995, specialists from the United States, Canada and Western Europe came to St. Petersburg every three months, and trained a group of 22 psychologists and psychotherapists according to a program devised especially for this training. Foreign specialists led the training while Mark and I led weekly tutorial and supervision groups. In 1995, the project culminated with the launch, at Harmony, of a three-year educational program: the International School for Psychotherapy, Counseling, and Group Leadership.

From the diary:

1992. Group with Tom. Presence of death. I want to die with courage and curiosity. I want dying to be interesting for me. Death is when all the words have already been uttered. When my father was dying he said to me: "Tsss, tsss"—the same thing he'd say whenever he was engrossed in something, focused on something, when he didn't want to be distracted.

Personality as orchestra. It has its scores, its symphonies. The conductor is Self. The composer—the soul. We are performing the music of our souls. It has many melodies and dissonance, harmonizing and polyphony. Everyone has his own requiem. Or jazz. Subpersonalities are the instruments. 'And one, two, three, four…' The choice and the polarization are necessary for the life of the psyche. This is reminiscent of a dialogue from Dostoyevsky, where there are no 'right' or 'wrong' voices, but everyone has his own truth that belongs to him alone. There are only seven notes but the music is endless.

We have a fundraising in Madison on the 10th of May, and after that a meeting with one donor. We are flying via New York. At JFK dozens of planes are stuck in a two-hour line for takeoff and it's clear that we will miss our connection in St. Louis. We have to stay in St. Louis until the next morning. The Mississippi is nearby. The heat is awful. Air conditioners help. The next day we fly to Madison. The woman with whom we are staying lives alone. She is divorced, her grownup children live separately. She has two cats and a dog. They have historic names. Mostly of presidents. The dog's name is Jefferson. When it barks at someone in the yard the owner yells through the window, "Jefferson, shut up!"

The day is very full: First a live radio show that takes calls from listeners. Then a lecture. At night over dinner a meeting with a woman named Mary, who is donating funds to our hotline. The next day we fly to Boston.

Gregory Bateson used to say that in order to act we have to be able to interpret context. Schizophrenics are deprived of the ability to interpret context. If you were to name a dog "Get out" it would never know when to approach and when to stay away. Information is a difference that creates differences. Humans are the only animals able to kill and love with words. Psychotherapy constructs meanings. I don't say what I say; I say what you hear. Information is created by the receiver. What we say is data. We construct the world through language. It is constructivism. From this point of view there is no "objective problem"—there are stories. And they can be told differently. Assagioli used to say: "Problems are not solved, they are forgotten." Let's view a problem as a temporary solution to a situation, let's move the problem to the category of "helpers."

In order to allow the soul/essence of the group to become apparent the leader decentralizes power, expecting from group the optimal expression of group resonance to the "idea." The more mature the group, the higher the likelihood that this resonance manifests itself. The group matures as its members become more present. The more each member has the opportunity to be himself and to express himself—that is to say, to be present—the stronger the group. In a way, the leader minimizes his or her power and that creates a certain discomfort, because with the decentralization of power the level of uncertainty within the group rises. At the same time, the level of safety of the group's participants influences the extent of uncertainty, and the leader is responsible for the creation and monitoring of the level of necessary safety. Herein lies the most famous paradox: by minimizing the two former expressions of power, by rejecting them, by submitting to the unknown, the leader at the same time enforces the aspect of the group experience that—as it steadies itself against a possibly as-yet unrecognized idea—at the given moment maximally reflects the essence of the group, or, as Thomas Yeomans calls it, "the soul of the group."

Creating broad context is charged with tremendous force—that was how the school's program was created. The involvement of various specialists from different cultures, the input of ideas and energy. "Think globally—act locally." The context can be broad but at the same time the activity has to be very specific. Here it is appropriate to use Nils's metaphor that one must "take mouse steps:" very slowly, very locally.

July 1995. The Business Express Airlines plane has been moored at the gate at the airport in New York for six hours. Fog. "Some people just know how to fly" is the airline's motto, and in this context it sounds like a joke. One wishes to ask, "So where are those people who know how to fly?" Swimming in Walden Pond at 6 a.m. Warm, transparent water. There is something magical in this place. Fog. We are at Claire's. When I woke up in the morning I lay in bed and thought about how my life has changed in the last six years. Six years in this very house the changes began. The world of my relationships has changed, my life has changed, my work has changed. There emerged an internal direction, a pull, a focus on plans and beginnings. I am now sitting and writing, surrounded by people who are close to me, who are walking and searching together with me, and I don't feel lonely. I feel a sharing, a closeness of the soul, of the spirit. I feel as if I am at a certain point from which the departure takes place, and I have my bearings.

The Crisis

By 1993 my English was good enough to allow me to make my first translation. I translated into Russian "Lessons from the Geese" (some foreign guest brought to Harmony a short text signed by Milton Olson[28]):

1. As each bird flaps its wings, it creates an "uplift" for the bird following. By flying in a "V" formation, the whole flock adds 71% greater flying range than if the bird flew alone.
Lesson: People who share a common direction and sense of community can get where they are going quicker and easier because they are traveling on the thrust of one another.
2. Whenever a goose falls out of formation, it suddenly feels the drag and resistance of trying to fly alone, and quickly gets back into formation to take advantage of the "lifting power" of the bird immediately in front.
Lesson: If we have as much sense as a goose, we will stay in formation with those who are headed where we want to go (and be willing to accept their help as well as give ours to the others).
3. When the lead goose gets tired, it rotates back into the formation and another goose flies at the point position.
Lesson: It pays to take turns doing the hard tasks and sharing leadership— with people, as with geese, we are interdependent on each other.
4. The geese in formation honk from behind to encourage those up front to keep up their speed.
Lesson: We need to make sure our honking from behind is encouraging— and not something else.

---

[28] *Translator's note*: authorship of this text is disputed.

5. When a goose gets sick or wounded or shot down, two geese drop out of formation and follow it down to help and protect it. They stay with it until it is able to fly again or dies. Then they launch out on their own, with another formation, or catch up with the flock.
Lesson: If we have as much sense as geese, we too will stand by each other in difficult times as well as when we are strong.

I imagined that such a non-hierarchical, non-vertical structure allowed our group to breathe and move. And many of us shared this idea. But not everyone, unfortunately.

The end of 1993 marked the beginning of a difficult time in Harmony's history, which concluded in a painful division of our organization. The disagreements and contradictions could no longer be ignored. The schooner began to sail in several directions at once, the declared values were understood or interpreted differently. The disagreements concerned the structure of the organizations, its management, and its goals. Such a difficult atmosphere lasted for several years. These years were full of stress, conflicts, and, in the end, unhinged the organization.

From the diary for 1994:

I have been thinking that I am ready to leave Harmony in order to free myself from the "totalitarianism" of the system into which it is converting itself. At the same time, I want to organize a normal psychotherapy school with my friends. Want to do everything I can in order to give Harmony a chance to survive while at the same time to not betray myself.

From the diary for 1997:

It is possible that at the time, in the 1980s, we were united by the need to resist the pressure of a rigid system and in this manner there appeared a kind of a "brotherhood against" the system. The need for such a union at the time was high: to protect ourselves, to survive. This image, this idea, was supposed to create a space for collaborative creativity, which has been achieved over several years. Approximately five years. And that's not a small thing. And then the need for it gradually began to cool off, and everything began to crumble. Each of us has formed his or her own views on life, plans, values.

Harmony had developed through the process of searching, through the joy of collaborative free creativity, and these very aspects had seemed to us to be our main goal. In the early years our development took place in the search of a community and because of a community, which is why the splintering of Harmony was particularly painful, why it led to the division of the community. The Ankor-Peterburg recruitment agency, which we had created together to help Harmony to become self-sustainable economically, and which we had developed for several years since 1992, split from us in the middle of 1996. Many of our colleagues, friends with whom we had created our organization, left Harmony for Ankor, taking with them a part of Harmony that theretofore had seemed inalienable. We were not prepared for it at the time and this split left us saddened. I am talking about myself and about those who stayed.

Second Breath

The closer we are to events the more it seems that we have to control them. The farther we are from an event, the clearer we see that it is part of something bigger. Looking back, I see that that 1996 was the beginning of our rapid development. We took part in the Psychosynthesis World Conference in San Diego (1996); visited Natalie Rogers and Rachel Naomi Remen; met Willis Harman and Piero Ferrucci; participated in the international conference of the Society for the Arts in Healthcare at Stanford (1998); met with Thomas Greening, the editor of the *Journal of Humanistic Psychology* (after hearing our story he said that the history of Harmony was worth writing about); visited James Bugental and Irvin Yalom.

In 1999, a group of psychotherapists from our institute took part in a conference at the Helen Dowling Institute for Biopsychosocial Medicine in Rotterdam, organized especially for us. We met the creator of the institute, Marco de Vries, and his colleagues.

Over the following years, we participated in annual conferences held by the Association for the Advancement of Psychosynthesis in the United States. In 2006, together with Common Bond Institute (USA), we organized the international conference "Engaging the Other" in Michigan. There were so many impressions we needed some time for them to combine into a full picture.

Men's Group

Tom Yeomans supported Mark and me, and in 1996 he proposed that we participate in an annual men's group. He called it a "writers' group" because one of its goals was to discuss ideas and texts created by its participants. The group included our colleagues from the United States, Canada and Norway. All these people one way or another took part in preparing our specialists in the Concord-Harmony project and in the work of our International School. They knew our situation from within, understood what we had to deal with. Harmony was not only in a state of financial crisis, its government and structure had been disrupted. In a way we had to start many things anew. Over the course of several years, this group offered us tremendous professional, psychological and human support. For several years in a row, our meetings took place in Westport, Massachusetts.

About a hundred years ago, twenty-year-old Edward Yeomans got caught in a storm near the New England shore and made landfall in a little village called Westport, Massachusetts. Edward liked this place so much that he bought a plot of land here and built a house. There was a time when one could see the ocean from the house, but Edward's descendants planted the meadows with trees, and now you can only hear the ocean. Trees, bushes, and other vegetation were planted in such a way as to create reverse perspective: if you were to look from the house toward the ocean the tapering bushes narrow the space. If, on the other hand, you were to walk from the ocean to the house, the plants gradually widen to open the view of the house and a wide meadow that lies before it, with a large cedar in the middle of the meadow. A road runs behind the house. In this house Tom had spent many summers of his childhood. A sign of Victorian times: the house has no double beds (my God, they did not know the joy of embracing one other in their sleep!). The inside is dark and cool even on hot, sunny summer days. A calm and a particular beauty are present in everything. An old-time beauty with its smell and its swarthiness, a coating of soot on the rafters and boards. The walls in many rooms are decorated with the models of boats Edward Yeomans sailed.

For me, every visit here is an encounter with beauty and peace. I have my own personal story here: the story of friendship, of mutual support and acceptance, dialogues with friends and colleagues, meditation, walks, thinking… For me this is a special, sacred space, which for many years has accepted me regardless of the state I was in—broken, tired, happy… This space is our dialogues, long conversations, the hashing out of plans, communal breakfasts on the lawn and the most delectable dinners prepared in joyful company, guitar songs, stargazing under the night sky, observing the flight of fireflies, seashells drying in the sun, their ocean smell.

And the ocean! It is close, its presence is felt in the moist air, and even when you cannot see it, it is here. Before its gray waves we are all equal. I am writing these words with enormous gratitude and love, because in this place I found inspiration and strength for the next step, set by it the bearings of my directions and meanings. This is where I could freely and openly think, share ideas, dreams and doubts; here I found the people who spoke the same language as I did, the people who were also searching. Here I encountered understanding and kindred souls, and being here was healing for me. The point of encounter. Of course, this is my story, my interpretation of the local beauty and peace. It is possible that I idealize this place. For people who had spent their whole lives here it probably also was the witness to the suffering and pain that imbue life.

Fragments of thoughts from Westport:
> *…Being a teacher in a way means being a witness.*
> *I am simply organizing space.*
> *What does it mean to be open?*
> *How do I wound people?*
> *What is the benefit to us being from different cultures?*

Is there a universal culture?

What happens to me when I feel as if I am between cultures?

We are only skimming the surface.

In some Asian languages "mind" and "heart" are the same word.

The search for that of your own which merits spending time and energy.

Is there room for me in a group? If I could only be here in my entirety.

I can be here forever. I need to be accepted, included.

Parallelism and isomorphism. Isomorphism: a pattern that is present in a culture is reproduced in a group. Parallelism: changes in a group lead to changes in the broader life situation.

An internal voice says: "You are an amateur, this will be a superficial book."

I don't know.

Experience is broader than any theory.

Do I want too much?...

"There is nothing to be afraid of, or proud of"—Assagioli.

Rethinking. Internal work.

The last two years of the life of the men's group (2000 and 2001) we met in Maine near a small lake not far from Canada. This place is called Harrison's Pierce Pond Camps.

From the diary:

At night mice enter our cabin, and outside the cabin, moose walk. "It's better than the other way around," Tom rightly points out. Near the central building Tucker, the ten-year-old son of the owner, is playing with a snake he has caught. He shows us the "house" he's built for it. In response to our admiration of his skills, he promises to catch a snake for David Elliott. David suggests that if we have a snake in the cabin we won't have mice. Last night the mice ate all of his cornflakes.

We live in the wilderness, surrounded by forests lanced by swift, turbulent brooks and waterfalls. Everywhere here is the untouched beauty of nature, which is taken care of, which is protected. That is obvious from the blazed trails and the cleanness of the forest. The soul is at rest here. On the first night of our last visit here I had an interesting dream: a monk sitting by an open fire is telling me about the soul. He tells me: "Every creature has a soul. Every soul is open to love." This phrase lives within me for a long time afterward, it sounds inside me like a song.

But something important for me stayed behind in Westport. I did not feel a part of this new place.

Support

In the beginning of the 1990s, my colleagues at Harmony and I became friends with Mark Horowitz and Abby Seixas. Mark and Abby are friends of Tom and Anne Yeomans. Mark Horowitz is a sociologist, family therapist, organizational development consultant, co-director of New Context Coaching, and founder and president of the charitable Uniterra Foundation. Mark and I are close friends. For many years he has been supporting and coaching the staff at Harmony. Together we analyze our successes and failures, share our doubts and concerns. Since the late 1990s, he has been holding annual workshops at Harmony. Abby is a psychotherapist. Her hobby is calligraphy. Every Christmas she sends us wonderful cards, some of which now decorate my bookshelves: "When you come to the edge of all the light you have / And take the first step into the darkness of the unknown / You must believe one of two things will happen: / There will be something solid for you to stand upon / or, you will be taught how to fly." That's Patrick Overton. And another: "Where there is no love, put love—and you will find love." That's St. John of the Cross. Back then, in the 1990s, to support Harmony financially Abby started the Harmony Jar, a large glass jar inscribed with calligraphy. She used "The Harmony Jar" to collect money for Harmony's needs.

Together with Tom and Anne, Mark and Abby started a group called Friends of Harmony, which has been supporting us for many years. Why did they do that? I have asked them. Perhaps our work in Russia was making possible something that once upon a time they themselves had been unable to achieve in the United States.

It was Mark Horowitz who organized, raised the money for, and accompanied the Harmony staff to Amsterdam to meet his friend, Marco de Vries and to visit the institute Marco had founded. Mark thought such a meeting might be mutually inspiring for the two organizations. Marco de Vries told me how the name of the Helen Dowling Institute came to be. It is named after a London violin player who once turned to Marco for counseling. She had cancer, she was at death's door, and somehow she had learned that Marco practiced psychotherapy with oncological patients. Marco flew to see her in London several times; then she died. Sometime later at Marco's house the phone rang. It was Yehudi Menuhin, the world-famous violinist and conductor, a great musician who was visiting the Netherlands. He announced that he had come to Holland exclusively to perform just one concert, and that he wanted to donate the money from this concert to the development of Marco's institute—such had been the deathbed request of Helen Dowling, his friend and mentor. A Yehudi Menuhin concert is an enormous cultural event. The queen of the Netherlands attended, and all the funds from the concert were dedicated to the development of the institute, which Marco named after Helen Dowling.

Creating is impossible without personal input, without *giving of yourself*. The English novelist E.M. Forster has said, "It is private life that holds out the mirror to infinity; personal intercourse, and that alone, that ever hints at a personality beyond our daily vision."[29] The ability to contribute one's own into the communal pot is a gift that opens other visions.

I have met a lot of people (to be fair, I must admit: I've only met such people in my country) who sincerely believe that if someone supports someone else, then behind such support there has to lie some kind of calculation, advantage, self-interest. More than once, I have heard my compatriots say that charitable organizations and benefactors of all sorts act because of their desire to subjugate and enslave, and not because of the need to share, create and improve. In recent years in my country such ideas are actively supported and

---

[29] Forster, E.M., *Howards End*, Bedford Books, 1997, p. 84

exploited. I think this phenomenon has its own psychological roots. This is an expression of regression and dissociation: universal mechanisms of psychological defense, accompanied by the characteristic transfer of responsibility onto others. In this way, the source of the problem is external. We identify the enemy. And it is not us. The enemy is Them. There emerges a polarization, an axis of evil, which in different cultures has different names.

It seems a paradox that in a society that was brought up on the Communist ideals of common ownership there exists such a lack of faith in voluntary charity. Charity allows us not just to observe the course of historical events, but also to participate in them. I suppose, to paraphrase Alexander Hertzen, we need a second generation of unflogged intelligentsia.[30] So far it hasn't emerged. But we're working on it.

And one more point, regarding the most important resource that has been helping us throughout our journey. Once we had a gathering with the alumni of our International School, and one of the attendees asked: "I know why we need this group, but why do you need it? You're taking time out of your day and you don't have to." Her own classmate responded: "I know why it would have been important to me if I were in your place: to see these amazing people; to feel that the way they have changed, their growth, happened because of your work—to see the fruits of your labor and feel your involvement… It would have made me feel happy." He pinpointed exactly what I was feeling at that moment.

---

[30] *Translator's note*: Alexander Hertzen, 1812-1870, a Russian writer and philosopher often called "the father of Russian socialism," wrote: "Before the Decembrists could emerge we needed to have two unflogged generations of noblemen."

PART TWO

Facets of Presence

Values and Meanings

Improvisations on the Subjects of Commonly Known Categories

They say that whenever Baal Shem Tov[31] foresaw trouble coming he would go to the forest, to the same spot, and there he would build a fire, recite a special prayer, and the trouble would be averted. A generation later, when his student, Maggid of Mezritch, had such a need, he would go to the forest to the very same spot and say, "Listen, Creator! I don't know how to build a fire, but I can still recite a prayer." And the miracle would happen. Later still, Rabbi Moshe Leib of Sassov, whenever he encountered a similar task, would go to the forest and say, "I don't know how to build a fire, I don't know that prayer, but at least I know this spot, and that should be enough." And it really would be enough, and there would be a miracle. Then came the turn of Rabbi Israel Ruzhin. Sitting in his armchair he would grip his head in his hands and say, "I don't know how to build a fire, I don't know the prayer, I can't even find that spot in the forest. The only thing I can do is to retell this story—and that should be enough." And it would be enough.

---

[31] Baal Shem Tov (Rabbi Yisroel ben Eliezer), or Master of the Good Name. Founder of Hasidic Judaism, rabbi.

Someone may hear in this fable a story of how the sacrament of ritual has many forms. And someone else may hear the story of the inevitable impoverishment of every tradition. I hear in this fable a story of how the development of tradition, the bequeathing of sacrament from one generation to the next, happens not in blind repetition, but in the particular expression of a personal vision that is performed based on the ancient, with its foundation in the ancient. At the same time, everyone takes their own route, relying on the route of their predecessors and teachers. What at first glance seems a departure from ritual is a development, the next step in forward motion.

What matters most here is to preserve and convey the spirit of learning—a task that is different from simple reproduction and recitation of the memorized methods and techniques. A simple reproduction won't work here, nor is it necessary or possible. In this manner, icon painters in medieval Russia "refurbished" icons their predecessors had painted: they took the work created by someone and rubbed it with pumice stone, and then painted anew, on top of the old. This way the old retained its invisible presence as a primer, a context for the new that was coming to life. This echoes Igor Stravinsky's idea that an artist repeats in his own way what has been said before. "Refitting old ships is the real task of the artist," he used to say.[32] In order to make an individual step one needs support, something to push off from, something to lean against. And yet, the fable recounted above raises a question: what is the necessary, *sufficient* knowledge that makes it possible to deter trouble? I want to focus specifically on this aspect. I want to discern and understand that ineffable foundation the preservation of which is necessary and sufficient in order to continue and develop one's practice.

I would like to share what I believe to be the most valuable, the way of therapeutic existence that I have learned from my teachers and from my clients. Obviously I have not been able to master it completely, but I have been able to grasp a certain vector, to which I would like to introduce my readers. This vector, this direction that

---

[32]Druskin, M., Cooper, M., *Igor Stravinsky, His Personality, Works and Views,* Cambridge University Press, 1983, p. 79

represents the very heart of therapeutic relationships, is difficult to express in words. I understand that my task is rather complicated, and I am aware of my own limitations.

Nonetheless…

Beyond Technique

*"Out beyond ideas of wrongdoing and
rightdoing there is a field.*

I will meet you there."

Rumi

The word "practice" comes from the Greek word for "to be done." And the word "theory" comes from the Greek word for "contemplation." As a painting reflects the vision of the artist, so does a theory reflect the worldview of its author. Scientific theories are creations of a human mind, *speculations* that allow us to explain the world. But the world they explain is the world of the scientist, the explorer who created these theories, the world of an outside observer. Pure experience is impossible without a theoretical framework, the same way a scientific theory is impossible unless it finds practical confirmation. Practitioners may find in this a particular significance. Every specialist follows some model or school. And the reason is not that some are better than others. Every specialist chooses what corresponds to his or her own ideas about life, what rings true for him or her, what resonates in his or her own heart.

At the same time, it is important to remember that the instrument in psychotherapy is not the approach nor the technique, but the psychotherapist himself. A famous line comes to mind, "To a man with a hammer all problems look like nails." Imagine a repairman whose only tool is a hammer, with which he identifies. And he plans to fix everything with that hammer. Your light bulb has burned out?

He'll whack it with a hammer! Did you cut yourself with the shards of the smashed light bulb? That's okay, things happen, he'll treat your hand with the hammer. But it's not the hammer's fault at all. It's not about the hammer. It's about the repairman. We have no tools in psychotherapy other than ourselves. This is an important tenet. It is precisely why it makes sense for us to learn to transcend the boundaries of the *notions that restrict us.*

An American friend and colleague once shared a funny saying, "If you're going to buy a Cadillac do it as soon as possible." In other words, if you're going to do something stupid, do it at the earliest opportunity. That way you can find out as soon as possible that it doesn't solve anything in your life, that it is merely another illusion, and then it won't distract you anymore from serious business. If we were to apply this to therapy we could probably say something along these lines: If you want to master a certain technique, then do it as soon as possible, so that you can quickly learn its limitations and turn to the essential aspects of therapeutic work. By the way, the word "technique" originates in the Greek *tekhnē*—"to do with art." Art suggests creativity, a way of perceiving things; it means that something already *has been seen* a certain way. And now it will direct our next steps in expressing ourselves.[33]

What are, then, the essential aspects of therapeutic work? In his description of his book, *Family Therapy Techniques*, the famous family therapist Salvador Minuchin[34] points out: "In the last chapter, 'Beyond Techniques,' I wrote: 'Close the book now. This is a book on techniques. Beyond technique, there is wisdom, which is the knowledge of the interconnectedness of things.' *But by then, I think, the damage has been done. Technique has overshadowed both therapy and therapist* [author emphasis]." In a sense, these lines reflect the general situation in our profession: techniques have overshadowed therapeutic

---

[33] Heidegger, M., *Poetry, Language, Thought,* Harper Colophon Books, New York, 1971

[34] Minuchin, S., "The Leap to Complexity: Supervision in Family Therapy", in Zeig, J.K., *The Evolution of Psychotherapy: The Third Conference,* Brunner/Mazel Inc., 1995, p. 278

relationships, and in order to get to these relationships, to the very essence of the therapeutic phenomenon, one must first get lost in the procedures and methods. Possibly this is a necessary process. The Italian psychologist and philosopher Piero Ferrucci recalled that once, in the very beginning of his professional journey, he told his teacher, Roberto Assagioli, that he had come to a conclusion that psychotherapeutic techniques and psychodiagnostic methods have no essential meaning in therapy. That all that takes place in therapy is relationships. To which Assagioli responded, "I've been waiting for you to figure that out!"[35] Assagioli's expectation contained necessity and meaning: a new understanding has to come from within. You cannot force it.

But maybe it is possible to facilitate the conception of a new understanding?

Currently there are hundreds of models, modalities and directions of psychotherapy, including dozens that try to integrate different approaches. Rephrasing Leibniz, Roberto Assagioli once said that every school of psychotherapy is right in what it asserts but wrong in what it rejects.

Every school of psychotherapy is in some way legitimate and in some way limited. And regardless of which school, which direction you pick for your practice, it is important to remember that the therapeutic tool is not a psychological theory and not a psychotherapeutic model—neither of those are what *works* in psychotherapy. To a certain extent systems and algorithms can help to comprehend and structure what's happening. But they also flatten and simplify reality and, in that way, limit the therapist. To follow them rigidly may turn out to be an attempt to fit the reality into preconceived artificial constructs, and lead to ignoring and losing the understanding of the complexity of the processes that are taking place. It is important not to forget this.

I will use Viktor Frankl's two laws of dimensional ontology to illustrate this point. The first law states that one and the same object, when projected out of its own dimension into different, lower

---

[35] Firman, J., Gila, A., *A Psychotherapy of Love: Psychosynthesis in Practice*, State University of New York Press, 2010, p. 6

dimensions, portrays itself in these projections in such a way that the projected figures contradict one another.

The image Frankl uses[36] represents it in the following manner: two projections of a cylinder from a three-dimensional space onto two perpendicular planes that correspond to its longitudinal and perpendicular cuts, show, in one case, a rectangle, and in the other, a circle (see illustration I).

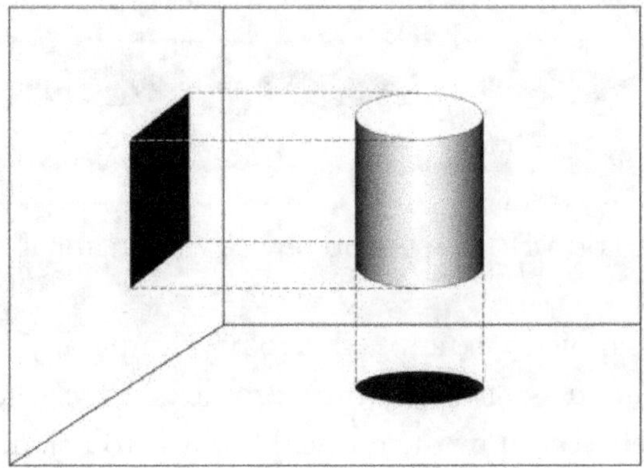

Illustration I: The first law of dimensional ontology.

The other law of dimensional ontology states: Different objects projected out of the same dimension not into different but into the same lower dimension are portrayed in such a way that their depictions are not contradictory but equivocal. If you were to project a cylinder, a cone, and a sphere from a three-dimensional into a two-dimensional plane that is parallel to the bases of the cylinder and the cone, then in all three cases the reflection would be a circle, as is demonstrated by Illustration II.

---

[36] Frankl, V., *The Will to Meaning: Foundations and Applications of Logotherapy*, World Pub. Co., 1969, pp. 23-24

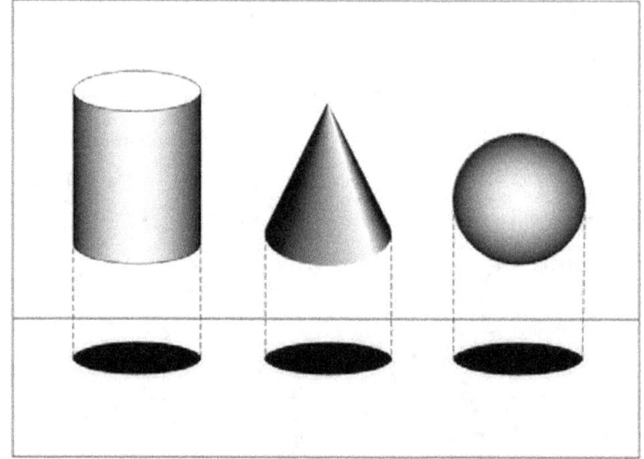

Illustration II: the second law of dimensional ontology.

Now, how do we apply this to psychotherapy and therapeutic models? A human is always more complex, more multidimensional than any model. To follow the model blindly is to risk reducing human complexity. Indeed, that is how every model is created: something is considered important, something else is ignored. The price for such disregard, for such myopia, is a distorted perception—and, therefore, a limited understanding of the other person. And that leads to inadequate psychotherapeutic actions.

What we know is never enough. The way out of this inevitability is to recognize the limitations that accompany every model, and to preserve our own openness to the new, the unknown.

Evaluating Effectiveness: Theory and Practice

Every school develops. Different directions connect, intersect. Reformers replace the orthodox. Ships are rebuilt. Representatives of various schools and directions often accuse the others of being ineffective, but no one has precise criteria for effectiveness, they have not been developed. Is it at all possible to precisely evaluate the effectiveness of psychotherapy?

Irvin Yalom recalls a case that put an end to his interest in scientific study in the field of psychotherapy.[37] While working on his famous monograph, *The Theory and Practice of Group Psychotherapy,* he had organized and carried out a lot of studies and experiments, and published the results in many scientific magazines. Shortly after the book was published, he decided to develop and carry out a new, significant study that would allow him to measure and evaluate the effectiveness of individual psychotherapy. He signed up a large number of patients and carried out with each of them three semi-structured interviews: one before the beginning of therapy, another three months after the beginning of therapy, and one more six months after the beginning of therapy. He invited an experienced psychotherapist to interview the patients. The psychotherapist's task was to focus on the patients' ideas of what they considered their main life issues and how they evaluated the level of dysfunction and difficulties that were related to each of these issues. Every interview was videotaped.

---

[37] Josselson, R., *Irvin D. Yalom: On Psychotherapy and the Human Condition,* Jorge Pinto Books Inc., 2007, pp. 44-45

Yalom also selected a group of accomplished therapists to participate in this study. Each of them had 10 or 15 years' work experience and among them were the most famous professionals who practiced in the vicinity of Stanford University. Each had agreed to come and watch all the sets of three videotaped interviews in order to professionally evaluate the level to which the patients' problems manifested themselves before therapy and three and six months into therapy. Yalom had placed great hopes on this study, and the experts he had selected were not simply great specialists—they were the best of the best. But the unexpected happened. The individual assessments of the experts did not correlate with one another at all: what some saw as progress others considered the lack of forward movement, and others still a deterioration, and so on. It was simply uncanny. One couldn't even think about publishing such results. Not a single scientific publication would be willing to print the results of such a "failed" experiment. But Yalom says that this was the first time in his research history when he trusted the results—and lost interest in scientific studies. Instead he became interested in writing psychotherapeutic novels that help readers to immerse in the inner worlds of a client and a psychotherapist, and, in that way, to study therapeutic relationships from within.

In mid-1990s, I read the following story in the foreword to a book on psychotherapy that had just come out: Two friends meet after a long separation. One of them is teaching at the department of psychology where the two once were classmates, and the other comes to visit him at their alma mater. It is finals week. The visitor picks up a few exam questions and exclaims, "Check this out, still the same questions!" "Yes, still the same questions, but different answers," responds his professor friend.

I suppose the author intended this anecdote to illustrate the changes that were taking place in domestic psychotherapy. The story struck me as very sad because so often the questions are more important than the answers. Knowing how to ask questions is directly related to the important and, at first glance, seemingly simple ability of the psychotherapist to see the obvious. "[W]hat one learnt depended not merely on what turned up in one's trenches but also on what questions one was asking: so that a man who was asking questions of one kind learnt one kind of thing from a piece of digging which to another man revealed something different, to a third something illusory, and to a fourth nothing at all."[38]

Let us compare the ways of seeing that are customary for scientific psychology and psychotherapy. Like any science, psychology relies on experiment or research. Experiments and research, in turn, rely on *patterns that exists in nature.* Supposedly these patterns exist somewhere outside us—"out there, in nature" (among patients and clients, for example), and we can study them from somewhere "here." Moreover, science studies facts based on individual samples. In geology it is a sample of a rock; in linguistics, an excerpt; in scientific psychology, the results of a study conducted using specific methods. The objects are different in different disciplines. But what the linguist and the geologist have in common is the consequent generalization and the transfer of the qualities of the sample (or of a certain selection of samples) onto an entire class of phenomena or objects. Each natural science has its own theories on how to perform this transfer, and it uses these theories to answer the question *why* the experiment or the study led to such results. In science such a result is considered objective.

The science of psychology can search for answers to questions about which kinds of emotional reactions take place under one or another set of circumstances, what are the particularities of visual thinking; it can study the patterns of visual perception. These are abstract questions. Answers to these questions will apply equally to anyone. Science works with concepts that are too general to apply to what Carl Jung called "the subjective variety of an individual life."[39] Science does not and cannot pose the question "Who is Peter?" because Peter is not a scientific problem. But in the course of therapy such a question can be posed. And is this not the most important question for Peter? Is it not through the understanding of self, of one's

---

[38] Collingwood, R.G., *An Autobiography and Other Writings,* Oxford University Press, 2013, pp. 24-25

[39] Jung, C., *Memories, Dreams, Reflections,* Vintage, 1989, p. 3

own internal world, that the external world opens to a person? Helping to discover oneself, new facets within oneself, establishing new relationships with oneself and, through that, with the world—that is precisely what psychotherapy does.[40]

Everything that takes place in therapy takes place within relationships, therapeutic relationships. And the psychotherapist, regardless of which school he or she belongs to, is not a specialist in the field of solving problems; the psychotherapist is a specialist in the field of building helpful, therapeutic relationships—a specialist who is present in the relationship. This is broader than any technique or method; it is, rather, a *tenet*. This tenet lies beyond techniques, it transcends their boundaries. That may be why it often escapes our field of vision, and although specialists from many schools and therapeutic directions share it formally and write and talk about it, in practice (this is particularly relevant to the process of educating specialists), it is often not given the attention it is due. Besides, it is difficult to express and describe.

---

[40] In his book *Design for the Brain* W. Ross Ashby writes: "Science deals, and can only deal, with what one man can *demonstrate* to another. Vivid though consciousness may be to its possessor, there is as yet no method known by which he can demonstrate his experience to another. And until such a method, or its equivalent, is found, the facts of consciousness cannot be used in scientific method." (Ashby, W.R., *Design for a Brain*, Chapman & Hall, 1960, p. 12) This was written in the middle of the 20th century!

Helping Relationships: What to Learn?

What are "helping relationships?" Let's take a look specifically at our personal experience. I often suggest that participants of my workshops and training sessions take part in the following exercise.[41] I'd like to invite you to try it right now. For obvious reasons, I will not suggest that you close your eyes, as I would have if we were together in a training space. But I think it makes sense to read the text below slowly, taking note of the emotions you experience in the process.

Sit comfortably, close your eyes, and let your mind wander freely through your life, travel back to your very childhood and then float freely through your life. Let the memories and images come and go until you come across the time when a problem appeared in your life. Not just any problem but the problem that made you feel as if something were wrong with you, something was not the way it should have been. You understand quite well what that means: You have too much of something, too little of something else; you are unable to make a decision to do something or you can't stop doing things that ought to be stopped; you can't change the way you are.

Take your time. Don't worry if you encounter not one such memory but several. Allow yourself to stay with these images until one of them stands out more. Pick the one that seems more prominent and stay with it. It is possible that other people already have told you about this "problem," this "flaw," as they tried to alter you. Or you may have tried hiding it from the eyes of others, hoping that nobody would know about your secret. Try to feel as

---

[41] See: Wheeler, G., *Beyond Individualism*, Gestalt Press, 2000

deeply as possible what it is like to be yourself in that situation. Which feelings arise when that happens? What are the sensations in your body?

When you determine that you have recreated that memory, open your eyes and write a few sentences describing your problem. What was it? How old were you when you encountered it? What did you feel when you encountered it? When describing your situation use the present tense, as if it were all happening at the moment. Note that you are doing it only for yourself and you won't need to share your notes with anyone.

Now put your notes aside, sit comfortably, and close your eyes again… And again, focus on the way that experience resonates in your feelings, in your body. Stay with it for a while so your feelings and physical sensations come back, so you can physically feel them.

And now imagine what would happen if you shared this experience with another person, now, in this present moment. Imagine that you are telling someone else about this experience. Just picture in your mind's eye that you are doing it. Notice what happens to you as you do so.

And now I want each of you to ask yourself a question: what would I need from this other person to take the risk of talking about this experience right now? What would I need to receive from this other person to make such a conversation possible? What would this other person have to do so that our conversation becomes a true exploration of what's really happening to me, and not yet another one of my evasions of my own experience, of my true emotions?

And now I invite you to come back to this room, open your eyes, and take some notes about this, to try to answer these questions.

After this exercise, I encourage workshop participants to share their ideas about *what kind of person should this other human being be* in order for them to feel better, and not worse, after the encounter. I write down their thoughts on a blackboard so that later we can discuss them together.

Here is a far from complete list of qualities that people who have participated in this exercise have thought this other person had to possess: *this person has to be himself or herself, be open, calm, know how to listen, be kind, patient, alive; he or she has to be variable so that I can be not always the same with him or her; he or she has to be interested, understanding, loving, sincere, trustworthy, stable, available, possessing of internal strength, wholesome, possessing of life experience, dependable, attentive, accepting, able to listen without interrupting, commenting or interpreting, has to look likable, has to be compassionate, assertive, intuitive, not give advice, not scold, not be annoyed, not console, not persuade, not engage in wordplay and not be afraid; friendly, with a sense of humor, smart, supportive, with a desire to help, with a desire to understand, attentive to details, steady, warm, wise, strong, in step with me, able to keep a secret, oriented toward me, asking me what I am concerned about…*

What kind of qualities would you wish to see?

Here's why I turned to this exercise, although you probably have already noticed an interesting feature of the comments listed above: It's astonishing that although each time my audience for this exercise has consisted of psychologists and psychotherapists, not once did anyone mention that this other person had to be versed in any particular method or be an expert in any kind of approach. No one said that this person had, for example, to possess the qualities of active listening or crisis intervention, or be a certified specialist, a member of a professional association, or to have a license, etc. etc. Everyone agreed that the qualities this person had to possess were not in any way "specialist" but purely human.

This seeming paradox will disappear and the comments of the participants will make perfect sense if one notices that they describe a very specific set of human qualities or skills (proficiencies, as they like to say nowadays). If we try to analyze and summarize the responses we will discover that this "ideal" person performs the role of an ally, *on your side*, sees you as you are, and at the same time this person *supports your experience* without trying to influence it, accepts it as it is. When someone acts this way toward us we feel supported, we feel an influx of energy, our soul blossoms.

Another important thing that becomes apparent from the responses of the participants in this exercise is the inadequacy of a large portion of existing training programs for psychotherapists and practical psychologists. These programs are mostly focused on mastering methods, techniques or approaches, but do not teach how to build helping relationships, and do not care about the human or spiritual preparedness of the students. When I say "spiritual preparedness" in no way do I mean to say religious preparedness. It is absolutely not one and the same. I am talking about the ethical, moral, cultural preparedness, or, to paraphrase Gabriel Marcel, about the ability to open one's human wholeness and receive another into that human wholeness.

In the late 1980s, or perhaps in the early 1990s, the wonderful American psychotherapist and educator Arthur Seagull, who was one of my teachers, said: "The goal of traditional academic education is to internalize information and demonstrate knowledge. The goal of our education is to learn to be open to others." I remember how, at the time, this stunned me: Weren't it the others who were supposed to be open to me, and not the other way around?

Another American psychotherapist, Don Brand, told a story that happened to him when he was still a young psychoanalyst. At the time Don was working in New York, and among his early clients there was a young woman. During one session, she told him about what had happened to her after their previous meeting. An important thing to keep in mind here is that Don recalled feeling very satisfied with his work during their previous session. He was under the impression that he and his client had been able to make a certain breakthrough, to reach an insight, and the session had been particularly interesting and effective. And here is what the client told Don:

After that session, she left his office in a terrible state. She was in utter despair. She didn't know what to do. She thought there was absolutely nothing left in the whole world on which she could rely, against which she could steady herself. Almost mechanically she hailed down a cab and gave the driver her address. By the time the driver brought her to her house she was in tears, her condition was absolutely intolerable, and then she decided to ask the driver, "Sir, would you mind please holding my hand?"

"You know these New York taxis," Don told me. "The driver's seat is separated from the back seat with a partition that has this tiny window for you to pass the cash, a hand is the biggest thing that can really go through it." (That's what it was like when he and I met back in the 1980s.) "Anyway, the driver—a young black kid—stuck his hand through this tiny window and she grabbed it and they just sat there for a while." After that she felt a little better, she thanked the driver, got out of the cab, and went upstairs to her apartment. That night she decided not to kill herself.

She told all this to Don when she came to their next meeting. Don was stunned by what had happened to his client, what she had to live through, and how different her experience was from his assumptions. As he finished telling this story he pronounced, "What I, a professionally trained psychotherapist, could not achieve in an hour of work, that young driver—most likely, not very educated—achieved in five minutes." What exactly did that young man do? And what had Don not done? These are questions to ponder. But I want to point out right now one important thing Don *did* do: he told us, his students, about this episode. It is not very often that psychotherapists acknowledge their own mistakes.

In order to share failures and difficult experiences, one needs to possess courage and honesty. One must also possess a sense of responsibility for one's experience, for the steps taken, for the risk. The ability to respond—to respond in the broadest sense of the word, including to your own actions—is a valuable quality. Every therapist must see and recognize that he or she can serve not only as a healer, but also as a catalyst for destruction. A psychotherapist often makes mistakes, has doubts, is in a state of creative search, because one must learn how to create relationships. But it is never possible to learn this completely. A professional is always searching. He or she is taking note of his or her mistakes and difficulties, and looking for ways of self-improvement. To keep moving forward through failures: that is something that applies to every creative profession. Unlike an amateur, every specialist has something that he or she wants to improve about his or her work, something that requires effort and development. Only amateurs have no problems and difficulties.

Behind any therapeutic action there are certain values that serve as the basis for the therapist's behavior, his or her therapeutic practice. The roots of a therapeutic action are steeped in these values, and the therapeutic action becomes the external embodiment of these values. The reason *why* you are a therapist may directly influence what the therapy you perform looks like.

A Natural Process

At the basis of existence for each of us there lies a drive to express our true essence, and such expression requires certain conditions. Representatives of various schools of psychology recognize this. In his object relations theory, for example, Donald Winnicott stressed the role of support and mirroring in the formation of *true self*. Heinz Kohut, who developed the school of self-psychology, spoke of empathic stance as the catalyst for the formation of *nuclear self*. Jung believed that the goals of psychological as well as biological development are *self-realization* and *individuation*. In humanistic psychology, Abraham Maslow spoke about the drive to *self-actualization*; Assagioli, of the natural process of *self-realization*; Carl Rogers, of the *tendency to actualize, fulfillment of the potential*, and *growth*. Regardless of what we choose to call it, the tendency toward development, self-expression, the revelation of the deep essence is common for all things living, for life itself (let us recall Karen Horney's famous metaphor about the acorn and the oak tree)[42].

We may not be aware of this tendency, but when circumstances allow us to express ourselves and we are accepted the way we really are, we experience joy and fulfillment. In such moments we experience our own genuineness, connect with the sense of our human value; we experience the rapture of being.

---

[42] *Translator's note*: "You need not, and in fact cannot, teach an acorn to grow into an oak tree, but when given a chance, its intrinsic potentialities will develop. Similarly, the human individual, given a chance, tends to develop his particular human potentialities." Horney, K., *Neurosis and Human Growth: The Struggle Toward Self-Realization*, Norton, 1991, p. 17

This natural tendency, however, encounters mighty obstacles, which are also typical for the nature of human development. The development depends on the balance of many forces, and often instead of blossoming and developing the essence of our potential we become something else. Often we become pierced with incompleteness and lack of self-realization. Why does this happen?

It is possible that the natural process includes at least two sides, and the experience of destructive relationships, which brands our personality, also inevitably takes part in our development, along with self-realization. This may be a necessary element of the conditions for the natural development process. What constitutes a nurturing environment for the establishment of a child's personality simultaneously turns out to be the place of the child's vulnerability. I am talking about relationships.

The life of a helpless infant depends on the people who surround her, without them she simply won't survive. Her safety depends on them, they provide her with food, warmth; they may surround her with love. For an infant, to lose relationships means to die. What happens when a child is not accepted—and I am not even talking about circumstances of violence and neglect—many authors describe as *interruptions of the continuity of being, psychic annihilation* (Winnicott), *soul-wound* (Yeomans). John Firman and Ann Gila call it the *primal wound*. The "primariness" in the term *primal wound* points not so much to the early age at which the wound is incurred as to the wounding of a primary, basic, fundamental human need in I-Thou relationships—as well as to the universality of suffering, the inevitability that each child will encounter forces that do not recognize her, ignore her, are hostile toward her.

In order to hold on, to not perish, in order to be accepted by those on whom the child's survival depends, her personality has to adjust to fit a certain required framework, denying its own genuineness. To describe this phenomenon Horney and Maslow used the term *secret psychic death in childhood*. They are not talking about the literal death of a soul, but about a loss of this connection to this dimension of human experience due to trauma, and about the perception of self and of the world formed under the influence of trauma. This is precisely what is expressed in the anonymous letter introduced by Horney:

> *How is it possible to lose a self? The treachery, unknown and unthinkable, begins with our secret psychic death in childhood—if and when we are not loved and cut off from our spontaneous wishes. … He has not been accepted for himself, as he is. "Oh, they 'love' him," but they want him or expect him or force him to be different! Therefore he must be unacceptable. He himself learns to believe it and at last even takes it for granted. He has truly given himself up. No matter now whether he obeys then, whether he clings, rebels or withdraws—his behavior, his performance is all that matters. His center of gravity is in "Them," not in himself—yet if he so much as noticed it he'd think it natural enough. And the whole thing is entirely plausible; all invisible, automatic, and anonymous.[43]*

And it is not something that *sometimes happens* to a person in childhood. The situation in which a child has to survive, in which her natural need for love and attachment may turn out to be merely an ephemeral dream, and the need to adjust and betray herself becomes the unexceptional everyday rule that forms and nurtures a deep personal conflict, may persist throughout her entire childhood. How does that happen?

A colleague showed me an essay written by her eight-year-old son. I have her permission to quote it and reproduce it here fully, without changes.

The Dragonfly and the Ant
A contemplative essay

I read Ivan Krylov's fable The Dragonfly and the Ant[44] with interest and bewilderment. I completely disagree with the moral of this fable.

---

[43] Firman, J., Gila, A., *A Psychotherapy of Love: Psychosynthesis in Practice*, State University of New York Press, 2010, p. 40

[44] *Translator's note*: Ivan Krylov's *The Dragonfly and the Ant* is an early-19th-century retelling, in Russian, of Aesop's *The Ant and the Grasshopper*. In Krylov's version, the Dragonfly fills the role of the Grasshopper.

In this fable the bouncing Dragonfly has spent the whole summer singing, has not stored any provisions, has not prepared firewood, and then winter hits all of a sudden as usual. So that she wouldn't die of cold and hunger, the Dragonfly turned to a male, her friend the Ant. She merely asked him to "shelter and warm" her. And to that the Ant responded insolently, "So why don't you go off and dance some!"

I believe that the moral of the fable should be as follows: of course ants are useful animals, but there also has to be someone who flutters just because, for the sake of beauty, so that the world is colorful. I would have sheltered the Dragonfly, and I would have sheltered the Butterfly, and it's okay to share provisions, I am not greedy. Let them flutter because without them there is no spring. And no summer, either.

It is not merely a moving essay. It is a gift. The child has demonstrated his ability to think freely, to commiserate. At the very least, he has demonstrated his literacy. But not everything in our world is this simple. The dramatic part of this anecdote took place later, when the teacher, a young woman, summoned the boy's mother to school. She announced that although his essay formally had no mistakes she could not give it a passing grade because in his essay the child did not demonstrate the ability to comprehend the meaning of the literary work. "He did not understand the fable's meaning," she said. In this particular case, the boy's mother had enough composure to calm the teacher without entering into a conflict with her (that was not easy, how did she manage that?). At the same time, she supported her eight-year-old son who had surpassed his teacher in his comprehension and breadth of vision. (What could she teach him? That in order to avoid conflicts he must conceal his true thoughts? That he cannot trust his feelings? That it is bad to be sincere and creative? That it is dangerous to be himself?) The episode is dramatic, comical—and, at the same time, typical. It is good when there is a person nearby who can lend support. But not everyone has such a person, and even if they did, he or she could not be close by at all times.

A child's psyche, by nature, has the capacity for conscious or subconscious identification with those relationships and modes of behavior that best facilitate survival. A child's development includes the internalization of conflicts and contradictions, different ways of repression and projection. The mechanisms that best fit the need for survival and for internal stability are the ones that are selected subconsciously—even at the cost of losing other capacities, including the capacity for the more complete expression of the soul. Stability achieved at this cost becomes in itself a factor in the creation of internal conflicts. For example, in the anecdote I just described, had the circumstances been unfavorable (say, had the child not had an understanding mother who was able to support him), the directness, earnestness and creativity peculiar to the child would have been blocked so that he would not be subjected again to situations that threaten his very being. For example, the sense of shame and uncertainty can become excellent aids in the creation of an internal critic. Later on this internal critic, this controlling part of a personality, will become an obstacle that will attempt to prevent or to block expressions of spontaneity. These processes, naturally, will take place unconsciously. For this person, being himself will turn out to be an insurmountable task.

But in fact, the rejection of the gift a child carries begins much earlier, from the inevitable trauma of birth. The very emergence into the world is accompanied by suffering. The notation in the medical record that says "Cried Right Away" is a sign of wellbeing, and the obstetrician's slap often precedes the contact with the warmth of mother's breast. The trauma of birth exposes the inevitable duality of the very situation of childhood, which is full of uncertainty and anxiety. One can see in it a certain inoculation to reality, a kind of psychological immunization that leaves a permanent mark on the soul the way vaccination against smallpox leaves a permanent mark on the skin. That's what Thomas Yeomans calls a *soul-wound*,[45] what is wounded here is the connection between the child and the child's own soul.

---

[45] Thomas Yeomans introduced the term *soul-wound* in 1994 to describe an interruption of the wholeness that occurs at a young age because the others do not recognize a person's uniqueness, which leads to this person's loss of connection with his or her own soul. See: *Soul-Wound and Psychotherapy,*

This wound leaves a mark on the future development of the child's personality structure and impacts the dynamics of development. Childhood experience will remain with him throughout his life. The fabric of human personality is woven from relationships with those who influenced us, those we have "owned," who in this way became a part of our internal landscape. However, despite the fact that we can no longer change our childhood, we do retain the ability to change ourselves, our relationships with past experiences, to reconstruct our *I*, to recover the lost internal wholeness.

However paradoxical this may seem, the path to self-realization may lie through seemingly lifeless spaces, scorched by suffering and pain. A psychotherapist may become a reliable companion on such a journey.

Concord Institute, 1994, http://www.synthesiscenter.org/PDF/Soul-Wound%20and%20Psychotherapy.pdf

Following the Process

The concept of therapeutic relationships was formed by the middle of the 20th century, when researchers set themselves the goal of determining whether there existed, among the various schools of therapy, fundamental differences in the helping relationships of a therapist and a client. Studies carried out by Fred Fiedler in the 1950s[46] confirmed the hypothesis that, despite the breadth of the spectrum of existing therapeutic approaches, schools, and the fundamental theoretical controversies among them, there exist no core differences between how therapists representing these schools build relationships with their clients. Representatives of different schools have a lot in common in how they envision the ideal helping relationship under the condition that these specialists possess rich clinical experience. It turned out that, as far as their perception of therapeutic relationships goes, these specialists have much more in common than specialists who belong to the same therapeutic approach but have different levels of professional experience.

Regardless of who the client is and what kind of a problem he or she has, the therapeutic position is based on the belief that this person is capable of solving the problem. At first glance this may seem to contain a contradiction: we all know that there are many people who feel cornered by life, stuck in a dead end from which it is impossible to find a way out. Most often it is these people who come seeking help. The clients may not be able to recognize it but, in fact, the underlying cause of their problems is the loss of faith in *themselves* and their own

---

[46] Fiedler F.E., "The concept of the ideal therapeutic relationship," *Journal of Counseling Psychology*, 1950, vol. 14, pp. 239-245

strength. They lack trust in themselves and understanding of themselves, and have diminished self-esteem; it seems to them that they no longer are in control of their lives. The therapist's task is precisely to help the client recover the lost relationships—with himself or herself, with the world—and not to rid the client of his or her problem.

If the therapist does not share this position it will be difficult for such a therapist to create the conditions necessary to change the locus of control for the client from the external to the internal. This, for example, takes place when the therapist shares the client's view that the therapist is responsible for solving the problem. The very fact that the therapist agrees to accept such a role will maintain the client's belief that other people, or other external factors, are in control of his or her life.

A therapist is not a specialist in the area of problems. A therapist is a specialist in the area of relationships. A therapist will, together with the client, participate in the complicated exploration of what it takes to recover the client's lost internal relationships and trust in himself or herself; of what it takes to reestablish access to internal resources and to reintegrate anew his or her own life. This joint exploration will be accompanied by a process of internal and external changes, which will advance the client away from dependence on others and toward reliance on himself or herself, on his or her own resources.

Thus, therapeutic work relies on two hypotheses. One suggests that a client has an internal resource, the connection to which may be broken. This resource is the client herself, namely her own ability to change the relationship with herself and with the world. The second hypothesis is that therapeutic relationships may serve the purpose of recovering access to this internal resource. The goal of a therapist, therefore, is not to hand the client a key to solving his or her problems, but to participate in the recovery of her lost relationship with herself and the world. And if the therapist does not avoid entering the space of helping relationships with the client, if the therapist really becomes a true participant in these relationships, then the resonance the therapist experiences will become another therapeutic factor, and the therapist will become the therapist's own therapeutic tool. Then the therapist will be able to hear and contain the controversial aspects of the process, and to retain stability in the face of the uncertainty of this process, open toward the experience.

This means that the therapist must possess a *therapeutic position*. I am basically talking about a particular way of *understanding* the client, about whence, from which place (I am talking about the therapist's internal space) does this understanding occur. For example, if the understanding is founded in the therapist's personal experience (clients, by the way, often ask, "You must have had cases like this before?"), then the therapeutic response will be external compared to the experience of the client. The therapist will "superimpose" onto the client, dictate certain external conditions for the client's wellbeing. Conversely, a therapist's response that is based on the perceptive listening of the client's internal experience, that reflects the client's understanding of the client and the world, the client's own system of coordinates—such a response will allow the client to discover himself or herself, unearth himself or herself, see, hear, experience, connect with himself or herself.

On this note, it is necessary to remember the evolution of Carl Rogers's understanding of empathy.

Early on (1959), Rogers spoke about a *state of empathy*:

> *The state of empathy, or being empathic, is to perceive the internal frame of reference of another with accuracy and with the emotional components and meanings which pertain thereto as if one were the person, but without ever losing the 'as if' condition. Thus it means to sense the hurt or the pleasure of another as he senses it and to perceive the causes thereof as he perceives them, but without ever losing the recognition that it is as if I were hurt or pleased and so forth. If this 'as if' quality is lost, then the state is one of identification.*[47]

---

[47] Rogers, C., "A theory of therapy, personality and interpersonal relationships as developed in the client-centered framework," In (ed.) S. Koch, *Psychology: A Study of a Science. Vol. 3: Formulations of the Person and the Social Context.* New York: McGraw Hill, 1959, pp. 210-211

Later (1980) Rogers rejected the idea of a *state of empathy* and started talking about *empathy as a process*:

> *It involves being sensitive, moment by moment, to the changing felt meanings which flow in this other person, to the fear or rage or tenderness or confusion or whatever that he or she is experiencing. It means temporarily living in the other's life, moving about in it delicately without making judgments; it means sensing meanings of which he or she is scarcely aware, but not trying to uncover totally unconscious feelings, since this would be too threatening. It includes communicating your sensing of the person's world as you look with fresh and unfrightened eyes at elements of which he or she is fearful. It means frequently checking in with the person as to the accuracy of your sensing, and being guided by the responses you receive. You are a confident companion to the person in his or her inner world. By pointing to the possible meanings in the flow of another person's experiencing, you help the other to focus on this useful type of referent, to experience the meanings more fully, and to move forward in the experiencing.*
>
> *To be with another person in this way means that for the time being, you lay aside your own views and values in order to enter another's world without prejudice. In some sense it means that you lay aside your self; this can only be done by persons who are secure enough in themselves that they know they will not get lost in what may turn out to be the strange or bizarre world of the other, and that they can comfortably return to their own world when they wish.*
>
> *Perhaps this description makes clear that being empathic is a complex, demanding, and strong—yet also a subtle and gentle—way of being.*[48]

What caused such an evolution of Rogers's beliefs?

Rogers's ideas were influenced by the work of Eugene Gendlin and his concept of the process of *immediate experiencing* of feelings and emotions. In the 1960s and 1970s, as part of Chicago University's research program, Gendlin and his colleagues were developing an approach he later laid out in his book *Focusing*[49]. In his studies of various forms of therapy, from the classical to the ultra-modern, he

---

[48] Rogers, C., *A Way of Being*, Houghton Mifflin, 1980, pp. 142-143
[49] Gendlin, E., *Focusing*, Bantam Books, 1978

essentially was seeking an answer to the question: why is psychotherapy not always effective, why is it that so often therapists cannot help people achieve desired results? He concluded that the issue was not that some psychotherapeutic techniques were better or worse than others. What was important was not what the patients were saying but *how* they were saying it. Successful patients turned out to be more capable of perceiving and reflecting certain internal changes. According to Gendlin's beliefs, a human body experiences a constant flow of feelings and sensations, and a person can refer to this flow over and over, making it a point of reference in order to discover the meaning of these feelings and sensations. Gendlin called it *felt sense.* Here it is important to consider the meaning of the word "sense." It can mean "feeling"—but also "perception," and "emotions," and "mind," and "consciousness," and "meaning." All these words are contained within the word "sense," and it is important to keep that in mind in order to understand the meaning of the term *felt sense*. Gendlin talks about a particular experience of perceiving a bodily sensation, which is perceived as imbued with a certain personal sense, a sense that has more meaning than a regular feeling or sensation. By the way, when Rogers (1980) and Ken Wilber (2000)[50] refer to Gendlin's works and underscore the importance of the phenomenon Gendlin discovered, they use the term *felt meaning* instead of *felt sense*. Gendlin's realization would not have become a discovery had he not noted the banal fact that a person is likely to experience and notice his or her own bodily experience. But Gendlin managed to demonstrate that a person has a direct ability to access the space where the bodily and the psychic are not yet separate, the ability to come into contact with "a zone between bodily feelings and mental concept." (This phenomenon of *felt sense* is fundamentally different from the phenomenon of bodily sensations to which many other therapeutic techniques, such as, for example, progressive relaxation and autogenic training, refer.)

Rogers and Gendlin agreed that *a person experiences a constant flow of sensations and feelings* to which he turns again and again *in order to discover*

---

[50] Wilber, K., *Integral Psychology: Consciousness, Spirit, Psychology, Therapy,* Shambala Publications, 2000, p. 244

the meaning of these sensations. These conceptual findings allowed Rogers (1980) to talk about empathy as a process, to dismiss the concept of a *state of empathy.* The aspect of motion here is very important. The task of therapeutic perceptive listening consists of *being sensitive, moment by moment, to the changing felt meanings which flow in this other person; frequently checking in with the person as to the accuracy of your sensings and being guided by the responses you receive; helping the other to focus on this useful type of referent, to experience the meanings more fully, and to go deeper in the experiencing.*

At the end of the 1990s, I had an opportunity to meet James Bugental, one of the founders of the existential-humanistic approach in psychotherapy. He is also one of the founders and the first president of the American Association for Humanistic Psychology. He was 83 years old at the time, and he was sitting in his tiny office in San Francisco writing two books at once. One was called *Psychotherapy Is Not What You Think.* The title was the idea of his wife, Elizabeth. She is also a psychotherapist. The title is a pun: on the one hand, psychotherapy is something broader then what we think it is; on the other hand, psychotherapy is not at all about what we think but, rather, about what we experience. Experiencing: psychotherapy is geared precisely toward the realization of the changes of what we are experiencing. Bugental explained his idea very simply. He would ask me: "What are you experiencing right now?," "And what are you experiencing now?," and he would point out the dynamic, the changing flow of the felt senses. In this way, he referred to my potential to come in touch with my own experience, to come in touch with myself.

Some psychoanalytically-minded psychotherapists—for example, Leston Havens and Kohut—make a clear distinction between *empathy* and *intuition.* Havens believes[51] that what defines the difference is the choice of place in which the therapist chooses to put himself or herself: with *the other* or with the *self.* Therein, inside his own mind, lies the practical difference between empathy and intuition. Havens uses terms he borrows from M.F. Shore, distinguishing between *self-effacing empathy*

---

[51] Havens, L., "Explorations in the Uses of Language in Psychotherapy: Complex Empathic Statement," *The American Journal of Psychiatry,* 1979, vol. 42, p. 40-44

and *self-involving empathy*. This principal difference depends on whether the therapist, in order to penetrate the internal world of the client, is trying to "set himself aside," or if he is projecting himself onto the client. In his therapeutic work Havens uses only self-effacing empathy.

The nature of feelings is complex and their spectrum is incomparably richer than the existing names of emotions. Often only poetry or music are capable of expressing the complexity of the states that do not have specific equivalents in language. And yet, in therapy it is necessary to use empathic expressions. Not only do they allow the therapist to communicate a client's state or reflect his or her understanding of it, but they also are metaphors that reflect sensations and vessels that contain it. They create a holding environment and an integrating force for the client.

An example of such a metaphor may be an observation made almost a century ago by the French philosopher Gabriel Marcel:

> *A few weeks ago I was walking in the Luxemburg Gardens thinking over certain familiar themes, when I apparently strayed into one of those badly kept gardens where everything had been trampled on and crushed and where no surprise nook remained to spur the imagination. A shocking impression but one with which I am admittedly familiar. The English term stale—a word which is practically untranslatable and which refers particularly to bread that is no longer fresh but also to anything that is repetitious or worn by the passage of time—occurred to me. Immediately, the experience I had just been exposed to took on substance through the efficacy of the word itself, became an object of reflection, then just as swiftly and as if by magic, I was free of it.*[52]

Today we would have said that at the base of this experience lies what—decades after Marcel had written this passage—was described as *felt sense*. Marcel calls the experience "an inner event" and identifies it as a "co-presence."[53] He discerns events (external and internal—thoughts, for example) to which we are merely exposed but with which we never come into real contact. When we come across such events,

---

[52] Marcel, G., *Creative Fidelity*, Fordham University Press, 2002, p. 11
[53] ibid, p. 12

we do not become open, we don't give of ourselves fully. A true encounter is a co-presence, *co-existence*.

On several occasions Carl Rogers was asked to name the people he considers to be his teachers, and each time he responded, "Otto Rank and my clients." He would never mention his professor at Columbia University—but he would name Otto Rank, whom he had only met once. "Rank" is the pseudonym of Otto Rosenfeld. He may have picked it as a homage to Dr. Rank, a character from Ibsen's *A Doll's House* who was besotted with Nora, who, in turn, was seeking self-realization and wanted the others to see in her a personality and not a pretty doll. Otto Rank was Freud's favorite student until he published, in 1924, *The Trauma of Birth*, in which he insisted that the pre-Oedipal relationships of mother and child must be the prototype of therapeutic relationships. That did not fit the model popular at the time, and Rank was expelled from psychoanalysis.

In the 1930s, he held many seminars in the United States. Rank and Rogers may have met in 1936 during a seminar in Rochester, at which Rogers was working. No one knows what exactly took place during the seminar, but one can guess at the kinds of ideas Rank would have shared at the time. He was one of the first to point out that in psychoanalysis a patient is deprived of his will (in Latin *patiens* means "suffering"). In his 1935 lecture in New York, he said that the psychoanalytical approach is focused on the therapist, while true therapy must focus on the client and the client's difficulties, needs and activities; a therapist, according to Rank, had to become the helping *I* of the patient.

Rank spoke of "relationship therapy."[54] He believed that at the heart of suffering lay angst, which disconnected the patient's *I* from the world. The trauma of birth is related to a loss of the connection with a larger whole, with the cosmic, the universal. Angst disappears only when *I* becomes part of a larger whole (in love, in art), when there arises a *Thou*, and through this relationship with *Thou*, the angst dissipates. "In love and through love, whether it be divine or human,

---

[54] Kramer, R., "The Birth of Client-Centered Therapy: Carl Rogers, Otto Rank, and 'The Beyond,'" *Journal of Humanistic Psychology*, 1995, vol. 35, pp. 54-104

the individual can accept himself, his own will because the other does, an other does." The task of therapy, according to Rank, is self-development. Development: the un-enveloping, un-folding; the unraveling of the hidden, something previously furled, some potential. Rank spoke of therapy, of relationships within therapy, as a way to support the natural human capacity for development of self into someone the individual truly is.

It is possible that during that seminar Rank spoke about this. Rogers said that he literally became infected with Rank's ideas.

Internal Person and External Speech

Both the idea of an internal world, and the internal world of a person, have a history of their own. In the opinion of Nathan Schwartz-Salant, they took root in the modern world only by the end of the 18th century. "Well past the middle of that century, people had, for example, much to say about feelings, but these were not thought about as interior, as 'belonging to me'; they existed as part of an immersion in a group process,"[55] writes Schwartz-Salant. To study the process of becoming of a modern person's internal world it may be easiest to use examples from literature.

"Internal Man" and External Speech is the title of a collection of essays on psychopoesis in Russian literature by the Soviet philologist and translation theorist Efim Etkind.[56] He borrows the metaphor "internal man" from Jean-Paul (Richter). The concept itself originated in the 18th century, when language seemed inadequate to the task of expressing the astonishing Internal Universe. Etkind points out that the Russian literature of the 17th century typically externalizes all the internal, psychological journeys of its characters. To illustrate his point, Etkind uses *The Story of Grief-Misfortune* (second half of the 17th century), in which Grief-Misfortune is the doppelganger of the main character, Good Fellow, and the two travel alongside each other. Grief-Misfortune is the embodiment of Good Fellow's bad luck and difficulties, which reach mythical proportions:

---

[55] Schwartz-Salant, N., *The Black Nightgown: The Fusional Complex and the Unlived Life*, Chiron Publications, 2007, p. 235

[56] Etkind, E.G., *"Vnutrennii chelovek" i vneshyaya rech. Ocherki psikhopoetiki russkoi literatury XVIII-XIX vekov.* Moskva, Yazyki Russkoi Kul'tury, 1999

Good Fellow flew like a white falcon—
and Grief flew after him like a white merlin;
Good Fellow flew like a dove-colored pigeon—
and Grief flew after him like a gray hawk…

Good Fellow hits the road on foot—
and Grief strides by his right hand,
and teaches Good Fellow how to live in wealth:
to kill and to rob—
so that Good Fellow gets hanged for it,
or drowned with a rock around his neck.

Although turning a thought into a separate character seems, in this case, to be dictated by the very essence of the poetic art, it is precisely such literary device, in Etkind's opinion, that exemplifies *the law of exteriorization of internal life* typical for 17th-century literature that is reminiscent of folklore. This law is expressed in the way the characters' external life is shown externally using different devices, including "prayers, divinations, dreams, visions, ritual weeping, keening, laments and monologues, always expressed by the characters out loud." The internal state of the characters in 17th-century literature may be conveyed through gestures: "he walked into the house and collapsed face down on his table…" or through actions (for example, distributing one's clothes among the poor). Thoughts are described as descending from heaven, or as voices of icons. Ill thoughts and sinful intentions are expressed through visions of demons, and virtues through visions of angel or saints.

The same can be observed in the two-dimensionality that is characteristic of the Russian iconography of that era: the viewers look as if from above upon a flat surface. The three-dimensional painting that eventually will replace such iconography will not only endow images with depth but also will seem to invite the viewer inside the represented events. Similar transformations take place also in literature. Most likely the reason for this is not the intellectual progress but the change in the order of existence, the order in which things appear to our knowledge, and the related linguistic changes. Michel Foucault called such a phenomenon *discontinuity*, when in only a few years a certain culture stops thinking the way it had thought until then and begins to think differently and about different subjects.[57] By the 19th century, Russian literature uses *introjection* to reveal the inner life of characters, and the author (with the reader alongside) becomes capable of plunging into the characters' internal world. The interior life becomes an object of observation and description, and now can be conceived of in a different way than before. Alongside the author, the reader gains access to the interior urgings and the ways in which these urgings are resolved. He gets to peek at contradictions and can analyze the characters' actions. In this manner, in Russian literature there arises an "internal man." What had existed before, but had not been outwardly expressed, now can be shown. Now you can share it, you can reflect in it, you can discover it in yourself and express it outwardly.

> *"My uncle—high ideals inspire him;*
> *but when past joking he fell sick,*
> *he really forced one to admire him --*
> *and never played a shrewder trick.*
> *Let others learn from his example!*
> *But God, how deadly dull to sample*
> *sickroom attendance night and day*
> *and never stir a foot away!*
> *And the sly baseness, fit to throttle,*
> *of entertaining the half-dead:*
> *one smooths the pillows down in bed,*
> *and glumly serves the medicine bottle,*
> *and sighs, and asks oneself all through:*
> *'When will the devil come for you?'"*
> *Such were a young rake's meditations...*[58]

---

[57] Foucault, M., *The Order of Things: An Archaeology of the Human Sciences*, Pantheon Books, 1970
[58] Pushkin, A.S., Johnston, C.H., *Eugene Onegin*, Penguin Books, 1977

Pushkin begins his tale by displaying his character's *internal* process, and it is so intriguing that it pulls the reader in. The vigor of development is intensified by the fact that, from the very start, the character's internal and external spaces are saturated with *tension*: on the one hand, this trip doesn't promise anything good for Onegin. He is forced into it by circumstances, and everything within him resists it, opposes it. On the other hand, all these emotions fill the character's soul as he is on his way to his dying uncle:

Such were a young rake's meditations—
by will of Zeus, the high and just,
the legatee of his relations—
as horses whirled him through the dust.[59]

The story unfolds through the sudden *penetration* into the internal intimate world of the character, using metaphors to which the reader is not forewarned, revelations that seem as if they are not meant for the ears of outsiders. In this excerpt we first hear the internal monologue of the character; only later do we realize that this was what he was *thinking* "as horses whirled him through the dust."

In the 19th century, readers gained access to the subtlest details of the journeys of the characters' souls. Now they know no less about them—and often more—than the characters themselves, and in the meantime it is as if the author steps back and becomes merely a reader's guide through the complex internal landscape of the characters. The complexity, the contradiction of the motives of their behavior, become subject to research:

Again, just as at the first moment of hearing of her rupture with her husband, Vronsky, on reading the letter, was unconsciously carried away by the natural sensation aroused in him by his own relation to the betrayed husband. Now while he held his letter in his hands, he could not help picturing the challenge, which he would most likely find at home today or tomorrow, and the duel itself in which, with the same cold and haughty expression that his face was assuming at this moment he would await the injured husband's shot, after having himself fired into the air. And at that

---

[59] ibid

> *instant there flashed across his mind the thought of what Serpuhovskoy had just said to him, and what he had himself been thinking in the morning—that it was better not to bind himself —and he knew that this thought he could not tell her.*
>
> *Having read the letter, he raised his eyes to her, and there was no determination in them. She saw at once that he had been thinking about it before by himself. She knew that whatever he might say to her, he would not say all he thought. And she knew that her last hope had failed her. This was not what she had been reckoning on.[60]*

Such text does not presuppose an idle third-person observer: the reader becomes involved in the process of the internal dialogue that unfolds before him, becomes captivated by it. Because of this, the reader perceives the work of literature empathically.

Using the evolutionary tendencies of literature, one can trace the dynamic of the evolution of self-expression, and therefore, also self-perception, or the evolution of consciousness. "Literature is the consciousness of the people: in literature, as in a mirror, its spirit and life are reflected…a stage in the world historical development of the human spirit which it expresses through its being. The source of a people's literature is not to be found in some external stimulus or external impetus, but only in its world outlook. The world outlook of any people is…that instinctive intrinsic view of the world with which it is born."[61] Literary records reflect not merely the dynamic of the evolution of culture in general; also imprinted in them is the specific dynamic of the evolution of man.

Karin Juhannison[62] refers to some researchers' belief that the feelings of modern people are radically different from the feelings of ancient people, that in the olden days people did not know how to reflect on feelings (except religious feelings) because the primitive self was locked inside collective consciousness. In particular, she cites

---

[60] Tolstoy, Leo, *Anna Karenina*, at: www.planetpublish.com/wp-content/uploads/2011/11/Anna_Karenina_NT.pdf p. 690-691

[61] Vissarion Belinsky, quoted in: Plekhanov, G., *Selected Philosophical Works, Vol. 4,* University Press of the Pacific, 2004, p. 526

[62] Juhanisson, K., *Istoria melankholii*, Novoe Literaturnoe Obozrenie, 2011, p. 5

Charles Taylor's research *Sources of Self: The Makings of Modern Identity* (1989), based on the idea that the liberation of self, which enabled self-reflection, began only in the end of the 17th century. Some researchers go further, insisting that changes in the area of emotions were so radical that motherly love appeared only in the 18th century. It is very difficult to agree with that. Most likely what changed were not feelings, but ways of expressing them.

In the Western literature of the second half of the 19th and the beginning of the 20th century, works appeared in which the character's self splinters, and its internal complexity projects externally. That's what happens, for example, in Robert Louis Stevenson's *The Strange Case of Dr. Jekyll and Mr. Hyde* and in Oscar Wilde's *The Picture of Dorian Gray*. The multiplicity of personality is used in painting, for example, by Frida Kahlo ("The Two Fridas"); in poetry—Fernando Pessoa's heteronyms. He had approximately thirty of them.

In therapeutic work we witness the exteriorization of the internal life of the client ("I carry an impossible burden," "Responsibility is dragging me down," "Thoughts grip my head in a vice," "It's as if I'm split in half," "One part of me tells me something and the other disagrees"). One can see a certain poeticism in these expressions. One also can see in them a reversion to an archaic mechanism that is typical for an individual as well as for a culture as a whole.

Internal Multiplicity

I can trace the eternally elusive thread of my consciousness, the way my thoughts scatter or gather together, the way I am carried away on the waves of my dreams. I can use my will to focus my attention, but I cannot stop the whirlwind of thought. At least that's how it seems to me. "It seems to me"—that, too, is a fantasy. "*I am watching myself.*" Such a statement suggests a certain duality, as if there exist at the same time *I, the observer,* and *I, the observed.* Following the tradition begun more than a century ago by William James, the modern American researcher Ken Wilber suggests that we talk about *the distant self* (the observed) and *the near self* (the observer).

But that doesn't really help: now we have two selves, and which one of them is I, myself? Perhaps the trap lies in the language: in it, both are *I.* The one who calls himself or herself "the observer" or "the near self" is not all that unbiased. It is not some independent, registering eye. The way *in which* I observe myself and what happens to me at that time will depend on the circumstances, on the context of my life. I write and reread what I have just written. I make corrections to the text, I reread and weigh the words I use, I observe the response they now cause in me—and now, somewhat from a distance, I read this text, which, frozen on the page, stopped being my internal and became my external. Now I can relate to it, ponder it, maybe agree with it, and maybe not.

But at the same time this text contains a piece of me. It is *mine,* though it is already outside of me, and now it belongs equally to me and to the world around me—another dichotomy, as if until now everything in me did not belong to the world around me. As if there existed the world around me and also, separately, a world inside of me—my internal world, internal landscape, invisible from outside. The worlds internal and external intersect within me, and I am at a crossroads, and my *self* does not allow me to catch it, it seems to either flee from me into the external world through words or hides inside of me. That's something *self* can do—to escape the boundaries of definitions, to be transcendent. Georg Simmel said that life reaches out beyond its own limits.[63] It's like an extension of the Big Bang, when particles of matter began to move away from the unknowable center to create our Universe—there appeared heterogeneity in concentration of matter, there appeared nebulosities, stars and planets, and in their complex interaction life began. So it is with *self*, or *I*, which from the moment of its inception pushes off of *non-selves* external to it, or, rather, absorbs them, identifies with them or reflects in them, projects onto them. And now this continues in our consciousness. The continuity of life and the discretion of moments. The present is pushed away, it bulges and submerges into the past, from which it once again turns into the present, speeding toward the future.

Attempts to give definitions to *I* are futile. It is naïve to fix *I*—to give *I* a name. As it turns out, such labels define nothing. There exists a constant confusion between my *self* and the contents of my consciousness. Simply now I know what my name is, but I also know that that's not my *I*, that's what they call me. There is *I* and then there is *mine*. *My* body, *my* thoughts, *my* name, *my* apartment, *my* profession, *my* friends, *my* citizenship—they are *mine*. But they are not *I*. I can change my name, apartment, citizenship—but I will not stop being *myself*. I can stop recognizing my own handwriting, confuse my jacket with someone else's, but if I woke up, it was exactly *I* who woke up—there is no confusion here. I am not a thing and not a process, but the one who exists. I cannot become myself because I already am, and I cannot *not* be myself for the same reason. I can observe *myself* and *mine* (I mean my behavior, health, emotions, etc.), but I cannot observe my very *self*. Even if I observe what is happening to me, while I am observing, the subjects of my observation are my feelings, thoughts,

---

[63] Simmel, G., *The View of Life: Four Metaphysical Essays with Journal Aphorisms*, University of Chicago Press, 2010, p. 10

bodily sensations, etc., but not my *I*. My *I* is the observer. I simply am, and *I* simply is.

A client says, "I have never noticed this about myself before." Or, "It's as if something inside me disagrees with it." Or, "There is an anxiety inside of me." I ask, "Where is this anxiety?" and the person, after a slight hesitation (as if consulting with something) says, "Here," and points to his chest. There is no doubt that he is saying and doing this based on his own experience, which is expressed in sensations or images. And what's wonderful is that present for this are both his *I*, his observing *self*—and something that *self* is observing. At the same time the observed can be represented by an object and pretty accurately pinpointed in space or described. But it is impossible to describe the observer. The observer slips away.

In Western psychology the internal multiplicity of the human *self* was not only widely accepted by representatives of different psychological schools but also became the basis for many approaches and directions of psychotherapy. One can recall the examples of Freud's *id, ego* and *super-ego*; Jung's *complexes* and the *various types of self* of William James; Melanie Klein's *internal objects*; Paul Federn's *ego states*; Fritz Perls *topdog* and *underdog*; Virginia Satir's *personality types*; the *subpersonalities* of Assagioli; the *parent-adult-child* theory of transactional analysis; the *voice dialogue* of Hal Stone and Sidra Winkelman; the *parts* in the Internal Family Systems of Richard Schwartz. I am listing only the most popular approaches.

Philosophers have always understood this duality, understood that *self* is not a substance yet it does exist. They acknowledged that our *I* is imminently transcendent by nature, imminently because it is equal to itself and we can directly experience the act of its existence, and transcendent because it exceeds any of our attempts to limit it. It is precisely because of this dual nature of our *I* that we can rise above ourselves, look at ourselves and see ourselves, turn to ourselves, check in on ourselves—that is to say, consciously take care of ourselves, of our souls. This happens because there exists in our *I* the capacity for a relationship with ourselves.

This brings us back to the subject of relationships. It is impossible to think of a person outside relationships. There is no person outside relationships. Without relationships there can be no survival. Even the loneliest soul is not preoccupied only by the animal aspects of its existence. Even an author writing a book about loneliness is writing it for someone.

The Israeli philosopher Martin Buber noted the duality of the human *I* as it is expressed in the relationship of a person with the world, or, rather, he talked about the duality of the correlation between a person and the world. He said that because *I* only exists in the context of relationships, it is only possible to talk about *I* in the context of relationships and there is no isolated *I*. There are two types of relationships: the relationships with *Thou* and with *It*. Therefore, Buber said, there exist only two kinds of *I*: the *I* of the *I-Thou* relationships, and the *I* of the *I-It* relationships. Whenever we say the word "I" we mean either the *I* from the *I-Thou* set or from the *I-It* set. Buber called these sets "primary words." Hence the duality of the human *I*, since the *I* of the primary word *I-Thou* is different from the *I* of the primary word *I-It*. The primary word *I-Thou* can only be spoken with one's whole being. The primary word *I-It* can never be spoken with one's whole being. It is the primary word *I-Thou* that creates the world of relationships. It is because of this word that what Buber calls a true meeting is possible.[64]

Naturally, the world's leading psychologists appropriated Buber's ideas and, in 1957, in the United States, Buber met Carl Rogers. The transcript of that meeting has been published, you can find it and read it (you can also read multiple items of research dedicated to that meeting), but I would like to focus on one aspect of the dialogue, an episode during which Rogers says that, in his opinion, there is a connection between a person's ability to meet himself or herself in the multitude of different aspects of his or her *I*, and his or her ability to meet the Other in the *I-Thou* relationships:

---

[64] Buber, M., *I and Thou*, Martino Fine Books, 2010, pp. 19-20

ROGERS: *It seems to me that I discern one type of meeting which has a lot of significance to me in my work that, as far as I know, you haven't talked about. Now, I may be mistaken on that, I don't know. And what I mean by that is that it seems to me one of the most important types of meeting or relationships…is the person's relationship to himself…In therapy, again, which I have to draw on because that's my background…of experience…there are some very vivid moments in which the individual is meeting some aspect of himself, a feeling he has never recognized before, something of a meaning in himself that he has never known before. It could be any kind of thing. It may be his intense feeling of aloneness, or the terrible hurt he has felt…or something quite positive…like his courage, and so on. But at any rate, in those moments, it seems to me that there is something that partakes of the same quality that I understand in a real meeting relationship. That he is in his feeling and his feeling is in him. It is something that suffuses him. He has never experienced it before. Now I don't know whether that seems to you like um uh stretching the concept you've used. I suppose I just would like to get your reaction to it. Whether, whether to you that seems like a possible type of real relationship or a "meeting"? I'll push this one step further. I guess I have the feeling that it is when the person has met himself in that sense, probably in a good many different aspects, that then and perhaps only then, is he really capable of meeting another in an I-Thou relationship.*

BUBER: *Now here we approach a problem of language. You call something a dialogue that I cannot call so. But I can explain why I cannot call it so, why I would want another term between dialogue and monologue for this. Now, for what I call dialogue, there is essentially necessary a moment of surprise. I mean—*

ROGERS: *You say "surprise"?*

BUBER: *Yes, being surprised. A dialogue—let's take a rather trivial image. The dialogue is like a game of chess. The whole charm of chess is that I do not know and cannot know what my partner will do. I'm surprised by what he does and on this surprise the whole play is based. Now you hint at this, that a man can surprise himself. But in a very different manner from how a person can surprise another person—*[65]

(While the tape was being changed, Dr. Buber went on with his descriptions of a true dialogue. A second feature is that in true meeting, or dialogue, that which is different in the other person, his otherness, is prized.)[66]

ROGERS: *I hope that perhaps sometime I could play some recordings of interviews for you to indicate how the surprise element really can be there. That is, a person can be expressing something and then suddenly be hit by the meaning of that which has come from someplace in him that he doesn't recognize. In other words, he really is surprised by himself. That can definitely happen.*

But the element that I see as being most foreign to your concept of dialogue is that it is quite true that this otherness in himself is not something to be prized…In this kind of dialogue I'm taking about, within—that is that otherness that probably would be broken down. And I do realize this probably is, in part, the whole discussion of this may be based on the difference in our use of words, too.[67]

Problems of language. The use of words. That meeting made a big impression on both participants in the dialogue. It had been billed as a public dialogue of Buber and Rogers. Rogers at the time was a widely known American psychologist, the author of the client-centered approach to counseling and therapy. Buber was a world-renowned Israeli philosopher whose work had been a tremendous influence on the development of psychology and psychotherapy. A month before this meeting, Buber said in one of his lectures at the Washington School of Psychiatry that *dialogue* and *publicity* were mutually exclusive terms, and that a dialogue could not be public. But right after the public

---

[65] Buber, M., *Martin Buber on Psychology and Psychotherapy: Essays, Letters, and Dialogues*, Syracuse University Press, 1999, pp. 261-262

[66] Kirschenbaum, H., Henderson., V., *Carl Rogers: Dialogues: Conversations With Martin Buber, Paul Tillich, B.F. Skinner, Gregory Bateson, Michael Polanyi, Rollo May, and Others*, Houghton Mifflin Company, 1989, p. 57

[67] Buber, M., *Martin Buber on Psychology and Psychotherapy: Essays, Letters, and Dialogues*, Syracuse University Press, 1999, p. 262

meeting with Rogers, Buber said that what had taken place between them had been a true dialogue and requested the galleys of his Washington lecture in order to delete his previous statement from the text. And Rogers changed the name of his approach. Now he was calling it *person-centered approach*. It no longer contained the word "client."

"What I am is good enough if only I could be it openly." This famous quote by Rogers demonstrates that in his view a person does not always exhibit his or her true self. The work of both Rogers and Buber stems from the multiplicity of the human *I*. Rogers, for example, often uses the terms *real self* and *introjected self*.

External and Internal in Everyday Life

Once, in the early 1990s, Don Brand and I were sitting at a coffee shop called Literaturnoe Café on Nevsky Prospect in St. Petersburg. I took an apple from a bowl on the table and began to examine it. Don asked what I was seeing in the apple. I said that a lot of people in Russia believed that if there were worms in an apple it meant that most likely this apple had not been sprayed with pesticides, which meant that such an apple was better for you. An apple, for example, like this one.

"Nonsense," said Don. "It means nothing about pesticides. All it means is that there are worms in the apple.

"This reminds me of a story," he continued, "about when Ben-Gurion founded a city in the desert. Now it's a city in the desert, but before it was simply a desert. Anyway, he saw a lizard in the desert where this city is now and said, 'One can live here.' But that's obviously rubbish! He should have said, 'A lizard can live here.' What does that have to do with a city for humans?"

With that, Don reached for the vase, took an apple, and began to examine it. I asked if he was by any chance looking for traces of worms.

"I am," he said.

"What for?" I asked.

"To give it to you," said Don.

The apple became inseparable from the stories, a medium that filled our relationship with new contexts. Because of an apple we expressed the internal that otherwise would not have been expressed; the apple went from being an external detail to being an element of the contexts that had previously existed but hadn't manifested themselves.

An experience does not exist on its own. "I am I and my circumstances," wrote José Ortega y Gasset. An experience is the *experience of oneself-in-the-world*. It is *relationships*. It is a field from which my *I* is inseparable.

They say that when the visual artist Eli Bielutin worked with his students he used the following technique. Eli would bring a stool into a workshop at his studio, stand it in front of his students, and say: "You think this is a piece of furniture? It is not. Half an hour ago someone used this stool to commit suicide. Now it is no longer a piece of furniture. Draw it." And, indeed, it no longer was a piece of furniture: it was the site of a tragedy. And its drawn or painted image could not be taken out of that context. A co-conspirator in a terrible event, it was from then on forever linked to what had happened in its presence, with its participation, with its silent consent—even, possibly, with its help. To paraphrase Ortega y Gasset, the stool also could have its circumstances. It stopped being a simple painting, it became an image and from that image it could be separated no longer.

To continue drawing on personal experience, let's once again turn to an experiment:

> *I am sitting at a table and holding a flower in my hand. Earlier I turned on a recorder to document whatever I was going to say about my experience, and here is what it has recorded: "...I am sitting at a table and holding a flower in my hand. I took it out of a vase where it stood surrounded by other flowers, and now I am studying it. It has a long sturdy stem. Careful! It has thorns, they are sharp. Out of its stem leaves grow on short petioles. There are many of them, on the bottom they are green and fleshy, one of them is slightly torn (somehow this finds a response within me, resonates with something slightly cracked within myself) and, on the top, toward the flower, there is a single yellow dry leaf. On the bottom the stem is wet—from the water in the vase. Now I am looking at the open blossom of the flower. The petals are scarlet and yellow, tender, as if made of velvet. The center of the blossom is concealed from me, there the petals cling to one another, joining together, as if spinning in a kind of a vortex. I touch the petals, and they respond to my fingers, opening and then closing again when I let them go. I am astonished: velvet wax—is such a thing possible? The insides of the petals are scarlet, the outside yellow with scarlet veins. I smell the scent of rose. My face touches the cool petals. The joy of recognition. As if*

the flower has touched me also, as if both of us have touched each other… I close my eyes, the petals continue to touch my face with their cool tickling strokes. I feel as if now this flower is studying me, as if I am trying to reach for it, to get closer to it, to move toward it… I open my eyes again.

How long did I manage to "be with the flower," and not with my own thoughts, feelings, impressions, memories, which I introduced? How long did it take for comparisons to arrive and for my past experience to inject itself into my feelings? I quote from my notes: "somehow this finds a response within me, resonates with something slightly cracked within myself," "the petals are…as if made of velvet," "they respond to my fingers, opening and then closing again when I let them go." All of this I attribute to the flower: tenderness, a sense of being slightly cracked open, and now even the petals begin to open and close in response to my touch. I am ascribing to the flower my own reaction. To what extent was I able to preserve a taut connection, my attention to the flower, my receptiveness toward it, and my own openness without trying to project onto it my own emotions, my own identifications? Because when I pick up a flower, I do so while retaining all of my personal history, and it is very difficult to interrupt within myself the torrent of previous, contextually charged emotions, impressions, and identifications.

I must stop them, I must be centered in order to separate from them, in order to obtain a new vantage point, in order for there to emerge a change in my vision, in my understanding, in order not to confuse what my eyes behold (the obvious) and what at the same time takes place in my mind, maintaining the potential difference between these two visions, this gradient, that's what needs to happen. I need to be aware of what I am perceiving while at the same time paying attention to how I am reacting to it, so that I am able to differentiate the very process of my perception from my internal response, and not to merge with it. In this sense I can ask, "From where, from which place am I speaking?" When I say "place" I mean a certain territory in the space of my own life experience. I can say one thing from one place, and something entirely different from another. At certain times I am open to one thing; at others, to something else. My reality changes. The conglomeration of ideas and attitudes is a mirage that often governs our perception and our actions. In order to avoid this, I must be present. *Nothing can replace presence.* Presence requires a stability, an ability to stand by, to be present for, to stay close, to not leave, to not avoid, to not evade, to not merge—but also not to undertake: to *not-do*, to be. And that can be extremely difficult.

Therapeutic Balance

> *"But Job answered and said: hear diligently my speech, and let this be your consolations. Suffer me that I may speak….As for me, is my complaint to man?"*
>
> *Job 21: 2-4*

I think that Nietzsche's famous saying, "That which does not kill me makes me stronger," is inhumanly optimistic. Does it necessarily make me stronger? And if it does, then stronger in which sense?

Almost thirty years ago, I was working with a woman who had lost a six-year-old son in a railway accident. He died before her eyes and she could not save him. She and I worked together for a few years. At the time I had very little experience and a lot of doubts about my ability to help her. She was disconsolate in her grief. Most of the time during our meetings she was silent as a rock, and did not express her feelings. Her internal tension was tremendously high, but it had no outlet. From time to time she would take a deep breath, fill her chest as if preparing to dive into the deep, but remained silent. When she did speak she did so very quietly and laconically, as if using this air in her chest to push out the words. She was afraid that if something violated the fragile balance she would lose control over herself. She was afraid of the tides of memories of the awful images from the accident. Again and again she would see her son reaching out his arms to her and calling for her help, and her soul would begin to scream and rip apart, but there were no words to express all the pain that enveloped her, all the sweeping horror. Time and again her psyche made her relive the psychological trauma. The tides of memories periodically hurled her into the past, in which there was nothing she could change. By night, she had nightmares. By day, awful images intruded onto her mind again and again. She was tormented by her own sense of guilt, the very fact that she was alive and he was not.

> *"I die together with him many times throughout the day. How to get back there, how to fix everything? I wake up and it's like a blow, 'He is gone!' and immediately this movie begins, it replays inside of me on its own volition, and all the time the different levels of my emotions, color, sound—everything is constantly changing like shards of glass in a kaleidoscope, and the variety of combinations is infinite… I live in a kind of crepuscule, in the twilight of the soul. In the morning I wake up—and immediately the first thought is: he is gone. And I just can't get used to it. I can't believe it. Maybe nothing really happened? He simply never existed, he never died, he never was dead, he existed only in my imagination, I had thought it all up, it was all just a fantasy. I have made him up, he was never born, I am simply having a very frightening recurrent dream, it keeps replaying, and I think it's real. It never happened…"*

She vaguely recalled the moment when someone placed her boy on the grass, and he lay next to her for some time. He was very pale. Then she held him. Everything was in a fog. During the accident, she herself had incurred severe physical trauma. Periodically she lost consciousness. At the hospital's emergency department, where the victims were brought, a doctor told her, "Your son has died." She remembered saying, "I know." Then she passed out again…

> *"He asked me to help him. He told me he was dying. When such a small child realizes that he is dying and there is nothing you can do to save him— it's a horror that you can't describe, can't explain. It's some deep, animal feeling that cannot be controlled by the mind. And it is inhuman. He will never be alive again. It's terrifying, it's as if I had fallen through the ice. I want to crawl out but the ice keeps crumbling under my hands, the hands bleed, and the closer the shore the less desire I have to keep fighting…"*

Desperation is the lack of hope. Desperation has no future and no exit. How to live on? Why to live on? Does it make sense to live at all?

It is a terminal situation. It is extremely difficult to withstand it because there is nothing within you upon which to lean; whatever you grab onto breaks up into the ice crumbs of the terror of non-existence.

During the first few months of our work I felt helpless around her. It seemed to me that there probably had to exist a way to alleviate her suffering, and I simply did not know it. I would read my notes from our sessions and I wouldn't be able to see myself in them. Something within me prevented me from accepting the irrevocability of loss. I told my supervisor about my feelings, about what was happening to me during the sessions. And my supervisor said something along the lines of "Maybe you need to cry together with her." I didn't quite understand that at the time, but shortly thereafter I stopped by Dom Knigi, a bookstore on Nevsky Prospect, and, for reasons unclear to me, headed to a section that until then I had barely ever visited—the section with books about theater, film, ballet. I remember coming up to a display table and mechanically picking up the first book I laid my eyes on. It turned out to be a book by Maurice Béjart, the famous French choreographer, who at the time was visiting the Soviet Union. I opened it at random and read (as I recall): "There is this fable: they asked God the Father: 'God, why do train wrecks happen?' God paused and said: 'You can't explain a train wreck, you have to live through it.'" I remember leaving the bookstore absolutely stunned. Could I have expected *this kind* of supervision? This synchronicity helped me understand that my own unexpressed emotions were the obstacle in my work with my client; that if I wanted to practice therapy I had to work on them.

Nothing new here. Each time I boarded a plane I would hear flight attendants explain the safety rules, telling the passengers that in case of oxygen loss, oxygen masks would appear above their seats and everyone had to put on a mask. And that if there was a child or a disabled passenger sitting next to you, you had to *put on your own mask first, and help your neighbor afterward*. Because if you tried to help a child first, or a disabled passenger, then you yourself could suffer oxygen deprivation, and if that happened you wouldn't be able to help anyone at all. The same went for therapy: in order to help the other you had to help yourself first. It sounded so simple as to be banal. But all of it seemed to be borrowed from someone else's life, a life in which people flew places on vacation, in which they fastened their safety belts. Whereas for my client all the masks had been torn off. Her world had cracked underfoot, the world that at one point had seemed solid, that had seemed put together once and for all. And now it was dismembered, it had lost its integrity. Plans, visions, perspectives—the very landscape of life had become unrecognizable, it had changed suddenly, without warning, without any kind of preparation. And now she somehow had to connect with it, had to relate to it. Live with it. Make peace with it. Until then, in the fabric of life, there remained a gaping emptiness.

Weeks pass. We keep working. She begins to take notes, keeps something akin to a diary in a school exercise book. The first pages of the exercise book are taken up with a child's doodles—the drawings her dead son had made. In this exercise book she writes about her condition, about the events of her current life: "Went to a Vadim Sidur[68] exhibit yesterday—the entire exhibit is an unceasing shriek of pain. The sculptures are laconic and simple—and that makes them strike the mind, heart, soul all the harder. You process them intuitively, the meaning comes later."

Maybe this allegory describes her understanding of therapy. Everything starts with perceptive listening; the meaning comes later. She copies down a poem by Sidur:

> *I am crushed*
> *By an unbearable weight*
> > *Of responsibility*
> *No one had placed upon me*
> *I can offer humanity*
> > *Nothing*
> *With which to save itself.*
> > *All that's left is to freeze*

---

[68] *Translator's note*: Vadim Sidur, 1924-1986, Soviet avant-garde sculptor.

> *To become a bronze*
> > *Sculpture*
> *And become forever*
> *Silent*
> *Pleading.*

Perhaps that is what happened to her. She froze, became silent and pleading. The form hides the content. Her notes go on: "Both the reader and the viewer are always the co-creators of the piece of art that moves them, that touches their soul." Maybe she is talking about the togetherness of the therapeutic process. And she is right. I also feel constrained, at a loss for words. I tell her about it. And she responds: "I am afraid without you and I am afraid with you. I come to see you and remain alone, and I don't feel you near me. Like running in place. We sit together and go rigid. Then I leave, and outside there is an abyss. I stay up all night talking to you, and then slowly recuperate until the next time. How do we break this cycle? Talk to me." Her attitude toward me is ambivalent. It is like a gestalt exercise in which you are told to link together all the fingers and then pull the hands in opposite directions as strongly as you can. A ton of energy is wasted, and there is no result. Just exhaustion, emaciation.

"No matter what I say it is always the wrong thing, it all misses the point. I am compressed into a ball, balled up, I can't tell where my arms and legs are, where is my head, you can roll me down the road, except where to?"

Whereto? Who will decide the direction? When I ask her about it she takes it to mean that I draw away from her, withdraw from her, step back from her, and falls silent… No words can reach her. Only images can reach her. There is no truth in words. There is truth in images.

She writes down a dream: "A.A.[69] opens my skull and it falls open as if on hinges, and he sticks his hands into the folds of my brain, and his fingers bend like snakes, and his eyes are predatory, searching. A.A.

---

[69] *Translator's note:* "A. A." stands for *Aleksandr Anatolievich*, author's first and patronymic names, the common polite mode of address in Russian.

looks like the Gorgon Medusa. It is a wrong dream, it doesn't happen, it cannot happen, it won't happen."

This dream again shows her ambivalent attitude toward me. But there is something else. Everyone recalls that in the ancient Greek myths the image of the Gorgon Medusa is extremely charged with energy. Medusa was both a beauty and a beast embodying fear, horror. To look at her was to become petrified, to freeze in horror. Perseus managed to defeat her thanks to Athena's tip: you cannot look at Medusa directly, but you can look at her reflection. Athena gave Perseus a shield—a transitional object that allowed him to defeat the monster.

Medusa retains her duality in death. Her blood possesses both revivifying and lethal qualities. Athena gathered the Gorgon Medusa's blood into two vessels and gave them to Asclepius, the god of medicine. The blood that flowed from the Gorgon Medusa's left side brought death; the blood that flowed from her right side was used to save people.

Besides, out of Medusa's blood sprang Pegasus, the stallion of the muses, which bestows inspiration.

The shift builds, it does not happen in an hour.

"That's why an artist creates art, in order to touch the strings of the human soul. If an artist is true to himself then he always has something to tell people. And what can I tell them, it is unlikely that my feelings will interest anyone." It is as if she is looking for a way to express herself. "How to express the soul, how to express what I feel, because there are no words like that and something approximate doesn't cut it." She realizes that she has projected her own pain onto Sidur's work. Is it easier for her to turn to the external? Very well, then. That is something we can discuss, that is safer to talk about. You can lean on the external, especially on a sculpture. The internal and the external are not divided and not contradictory, but are a continuation of each other. Sculpture has steadiness and it has a kind of safety. It does not require words, it can express the muteness of pain. In sculpture muteness becomes visible, palpable. You can relate to it. Sidur becomes a transitional object or an external center that unites, supports, shares her emotions. That allows her to exist. Does she have any suicidal thoughts? Of course she does. Death is always close. It is in the near distance. But even death can no longer resolve anything. Non-being already has intruded into her life, there is nowhere to run from it.

It is as if she is putting herself back together shard by shard, reflected in the mirror of the world. She would go to a concert, hear a line from a song — "If they are sad they do not cry but laugh" — and write down: "That's about me. I absolutely never cry, but a knife is constantly wedged into my heart, and the moment my self-control wavers terrible images emerge… Unbearable." As if some moral verdict has been carried out, fate is punishing her, radically rejecting her, denying the very essence of her existence. She is full of the desperation of guilt and blame. She notes that she smiles during our meetings, and the worse she feels the more she smiles. She calls the smile "idiotic." At the same time, she won't look at me, she lowers her gaze. She allows that possibly this is because of her resistance. It is as if I am becoming one of her accusers.

"I am a little afraid of you, though now less than before, because, in my perhaps not completely conscious understanding, you play the role of a judge."

She is projecting the role of a judge onto me. But she herself is her judge, and in that she contradicts herself. I can talk to her about it. And partially she acknowledged it.

"You are a part of me, but the part of me that blames me. I feel guilty toward you, even when I feel incredibly pained, when I feel bad. Maybe I am projecting my conscience onto you, because it is hard for me to look you in the eye, and sometimes it is simply impossible, scary. I am afraid to see myself there. The fear sits in me, hiding, I am fighting it and I feel guilty."

Memory torments her and at the same time allows her to maintain a relationship with a lost whole. She is afraid to see herself, fearful of encountering her real self. As a rule she does not respond to my comments or responds monosyllabically. Whenever I bring this to her attention she responds by shutting down, and then an oppressive tension spreads through the office.

"I have two worlds—here with you and out there without you, and I don't know which one is worse."

This goes on session after session. It is easier for her to remain silent, to shut down in the pain and the sense of guilt, to not look up in order to not see, to not encounter something even more terrifying. One would think, what can be more terrifying? I am learning to relate to semitones, to the understated, the unrevealed that is awaiting its time. It is difficult to be with it. Because the essence of despair is that nothing can help. There is no way to avoid despair, no way to step back from it. You can get distracted from it for a while, but that only temporarily weakens its grip, which soon once more will display its inhuman strength. She interprets my attempts to simplify and rationalize what is happening as a scam and an effort to expand the distance between us, and therefore, these attempts deepen her sensation of loneliness and despair; they lead to her distancing.

I peer into myself, trying to understand what is happening to me. The first thing I notice is the sense of constraint and helplessness. I can almost physically feel a paralyzing constraint. I experience myself as being drowned in spiritual pain, a suffering that has no outlet in words. I cannot tell her that I commiserate with her because when I imagine her physical horror and pain I cannot find the words that I would be comfortable expressing out loud. It helps me to recognize and disidentify with the reactions that arise in me. I begin to understand that unconsciously I hold an internal tension because I don't trust my ability to express it without being ripped to shreds. I fear that releasing the coiled spring of suffering may lead to the loss of control over the suffering, the way a small breach in a levee can lead to its complete destruction and the flooding of surrounding territory. Havens[70] points out the paradox that a therapist's successful sharing of a client's depressive feelings will result in the therapist's sense of failure. A successful empathic response by a therapist to a client who has suicidal feelings will make the therapist sad, and the sadness will be accompanied by ideas of hopelessness and helplessness. The extent to

---

[70] Havens, L., "Explorations in the Uses of language in Psychotherapy: Complex Empathic Statement," *The American Journal of Psychiatry*, 1979, vol. 42

which he or she is able to be empathic will be the extent to which he or she will feel badly. As a result it is necessary to broaden the distance that will prevent both the therapist and the client from ending the work because of the therapist's growing feeling of his or her own inadequacy and helplessness. Schwartz-Salant notes that the main difficulty a therapist encounters in the face of despair is that entering this area threatens the therapist with the loss of his or her own identity.[71] In this case, mirrors don't work and lead to a merging with a vampire-like force, to living in depression. In such cases the therapeutic position must be more complex. It is necessary to ball up in a way to retain steadiness, to preserve an inner fulcrum point.

It is very difficult for her to acknowledge that she is shutting down from everyone. And then, suspiciously:

"And you must have seen this from the start. I spent so much energy on resisting you. I thought I was fighting myself and it turns out I was fighting you. Why was I doing it and will I keep doing it?"

In this way there gradually emerges a new theme that I, at first, interpret as her search for a tool of control over her life. "What have I done then, in the beginning of my life, that caused a chain of betrayals and bargains with my conscience?" She reads Borges, Sartre, Jasper, Karl Leonhard. She carries out tremendous internal work. Her diary becomes filled with thoughts and quotes. She ponders the Clausewitz's saying that "a short jump is certainly easier than a long one, but no one wanting to get across a wide ditch would begin by jumping half-way." I get the feeling that she is preparing for "a long jump," she carries out intense internal preparation for the next move. Or maybe for a jump. At one point she recalls Ingmar Bergman: "There are moments when I can wander through my childhood's landscape, through rooms long ago, remember how they were furnished, where the pictures hung on the walls, the way the light fell." That was how she approached a crucial threshold that influenced the future development of our work. Carrying out this work—preparatory in many ways—took us longer than a year.

---

[71] Schwartz-Salant, N., *The Borderline Personality: Vision and Healing*, Chiron Publications, 1989, p. 50

Further work, which took several years, was dedicated to the processing of her early childhood experiences, when she had to endure sexual abuse and a series of traumas that psychically oppressed her, morally trampled her, that saturated her with self-contempt and the sensations of pain, shame and guilt. Back then, in early childhood, her wounded soul shut down, became as if numb because there were no words to describe what she was experiencing, and there was no one nearby to listen and protect. From then on, her face began to break into a grimace that looked like a smile—it was safer this way, it was fail-proof.

We do not leave life experience behind somewhere; it can announce itself at any moment. To grow up does not mean to outgrow our childhood. The time of our life is not linear, it can lie in wait but it is always alive. It talks to us in different tongues with different intonations.

Soul wounds inflicted upon my client in childhood required attention and work. Unprocessed, they were heavy burdens on the soul, they shackled the heart. The monstrous tragedy of the loss of her son demolished the unconsciously erected levee that had separated childhood wounds from her conscious *self*, and she could no longer drown out the pain of her own childhood sufferings. Only now were they accessible and could be expressed. Maybe the reason for that was the deep striving of a human soul toward possibly fuller self-expression, toward the overcoming of the obstacles that block the natural process of self-realization of the human essence.

Once, several years after we began our work, she brought a photograph. A black-and-white photograph: a courtyard flooded in fog, a naked tree and a stump next to it in the middle of the photograph, patches of snow on the lawn. It is autumn, or maybe spring. Everything is naked, cold, vague. There are no people. There is a sense of a kind of abandonment. To the right, in the forefront, you can clearly discern the corner of a brick house with fragments of a wrought iron construction, perhaps a support for an awning above a door. Neither the awning nor the door is in the photograph. "It happened in this building." It kept happening in this building. Many times. It left an unhealed wound on her soul. Again and again she keeps sketching herself, she draws a wounded little girl. She sketches a lot and reads a lot. She keeps a diary, she writes down her dreams. This reflects intense, deep internal work. In one of her self-portraits, six years after we began to work together, her face is divided into two parts: one part is light, the other is dark. The light part is much bigger than the dark. Her drawings, her practice of self-observation, are evidence that she is in process.

When I ask myself now, decades later, what was the most important thing I was learning at the time from my work with this woman, the first two things that come to mind are the ability to retain stability, and to be open to another person. These skills are interconnected. Stability without openness turns into rigidity, and openness without stability threatens to become reactivity. I think I am better now at these skills than I was back then. But I am still learning them. My old friend Viktor Kagan expressed them beautifully in his poem:

> *It reaches toward you, it doesn't let you touch it,*
> *It drags its wing, it aches to fly away,*
> *It quiets down, it thrashes in the air,*
> *Blood from the throat, an effort of a song.*
> *A lonesome ache inside you is an echo*
> *Of a mute cry of a disoriented soul.*
> *But bite your lip—don't let a word appear.*
> *But reach your hand and hold your very breath.*
> *Just reach your hand. Don't listen to the fowler*
> *And do not weave a net of shade and light.*
> *Just reach your hand. Don't say a word.*
> *Just hold your palm out, reaching toward her.*[72]

A Zen teacher and a gestalt therapist, Bernie Glassman uses the term *bearing witness*, which suggests several things at once: sustaining the focus of attention; a directedness; an openness to what is really

---

[72] Kagan, V., *Molitvy bezbozhnika*, Ryazan': Poverennyi, 2006, pp. 141-142. This poem also has an epigraph: "I found the sick bird but I fear to treat it" - Ivan Zhdanov

taking place; an acceptance; a witnessing. In Glassman's view, every aspect of daily life can be perceived as a chance to develop these skills: all we need to do is to learn not to deny what it usually denied in society, to keep our attention on what makes us want to avert our gaze, to be with what is.

"The key to meditation of observation is that the observing subject and the observed object are not two separate entities. A scientist may try to separate himself from the object of his observation or measuring, but a student of meditation must throw away the separation between subject and object. When we observe something we already are this object. Nonduality is the key word."[73]

How do we learn the nonduality of perception, the seeing of oneness of the world? "That is the question," responds Bernie Glassman. "That is the koan."

---

[73] *Sutra polnogo osoznavaniya dykhaniya (s kommentariyami Tit Nat Khanya): Buddizm v perevodakh*, Almanakh, Andreyev i synovia, 1992, issue 1, p. 219

Openness to Resonance

Let's say I am reading a book on the theory of cognition, which says the following: …cognition begins from the initial stage, which is perception. Later, comparing different objects, we generalize, we separate the common denominator of these different objects, we create a concept. This is step two, etc. All the words are correct. But I can say about the person who wrote this that he himself has never cognized. He gives verbal descriptions of something he only knows verbally. And there are words for everything. Everything is covered in words. But if he himself has ever cognized then he, for example, at least would have known for sure that never does perception precede any concept—the sequence is completely different.

Merab Mamardashvili

Have you ever watched footage taken by a security camera? An institution, a store, or a bank has secured to its wall a video camera that records whatever takes place in the field of its "vision." Sometimes they play back such footage on television, in the news. The most stunning distinctive quality of such footage is the lifelessness of the visual. Despite the fact that the camera is able to fix the movement of objects with seeming precision, it is betrayed by an absolute indifference toward them, which we feel instantly. If you watch such footage you will notice a paradox: a security camera designed to be watching over its environment is watching absolutely nobody. Unlike a video camera, human organs of perceptions are built in such a way that we are constantly distinguishing the object of our maximum attention. Because of this natural ability to perceive selectively we can, for example, easily distinguish the voice of our interlocutor in the noise of a subway car.

But such explanations are the purview of psychophysiology, optics, or acoustics. From the psychological point of view, attention is an act of will that is impossible without the reaching of our soul toward someone or toward something. Our vision, as the Russian writer Viktor Pelevin puts it, is the layering of the soul upon the standard imprint upon the retina of a standard human eye. The extent to which we are able to see depends on our ability and readiness to respond to the other with our soul's fullness, and not to react to that other from personally unprocessed, and therefore painful, parts of ourselves.

It is morning. I wake up first, I must get ready for work. I step into the kitchen. In front of me is a table. In the light from the window that falls upon the surface of the table, I can clearly see crumbs. My first thought: "Great, my morning begins with having to clean up someone's crumbs from the night before. As if they couldn't have cleaned up after themselves." I feel annoyed, irritated. I begin to make coffee. I glance at the table again. In the morning light from the window, the crumbs stand out in particular relief. In the morning light, they are particularly noticeable. One simply cannot eat at such a table. The crumbs are so big, how could they not have noticed them last night? Why couldn't they clean up after themselves? While I wait for the coffee to boil I start thinking. I remember that last night, at this very table, Marina and Sonya—my wife and daughter—and I had tea together. At the time I didn't notice any crumbs. As I wipe the table I think of Marina and Sonya and I feel glad. I like to think of the hours we spend together sitting at this table. I think, what a joy it is that I can take care of them. The crumbs on the table are now a symbol of habitation, of a hearth's warmth. At the same time, I recognize the change in my state—I am no longer annoyed—and I become cheerful.

It is amusing to observe such a metamorphosis within myself. It's a start to a good day.

In this observation there is a pivotal moment, when I, annoyed by the crumbs, start making coffee and ponder my relationships with my loved ones. This pivotal moment is a pause. It is specifically this pause that has allowed me to see events differently. It is as if I have transcended the boundaries of identification with my own irritation, and it lost its power over me. A pause, a break that allows me to see what is happening differently—that's what's important. Meetings with a psychotherapist can, in a way, resemble such pauses.

Occasionally, before a seminar, I offer participants the opportunity to listen to a piece of music, classical or avant-garde. And then I invite them to share their response. You can learn a lot from such an experience. Sometimes you listen to music and you "don't get it." You feel an internal bewilderment or irritation—or maybe boredom, impatience, sleepiness. And you attribute all of this to the music. Boring music. Incomprehensible music. But in reality these are all *your* feelings, *your* emotions: it is *your* gloom, *your* bewilderment, irritation, boredom. The music is a catalyst, you attribute to it your own emotions. For example, you say, "This music is boring." But it would have been more correct to say, "Boredom (or annoyance, bewilderment, etc.) emerges inside of me." It would have been more correct to own your own emotions and not to project them outward. When we say that music is emotional, we mean our own resonance, not the actual sounds. When we listen to music we hear ourselves. At the same time, it would be a mistake to insist that our description of the emotions we have while listening to music is exclusively subjective. More likely, it is our subjective input in the interaction with the piece of music, what we were able to achieve during our encounter with it. And what we could not achieve.

> *"They played Beethoven's Kreutzer Sonata," he continued. "Do you know the first presto? You do?" he cried. "Ugh! Ugh! It is a terrible thing, that sonata. And especially that part. And in general music is a dreadful thing! What is it? I don't understand it. What is music? What does it do? And why does it do what it does? They say music exalts the soul. Nonsense, it is*

not true! It has an effect, an awful effect—I am speaking of myself—but not of an exalting kind. It has neither an exalting nor a debasing effect but it produces agitation. How can I put it? Music makes me forget myself, my real position; it transports me to some other position not my own. Under the influence of music it seems to me that I feel what I do not really feel, that I understand what I do not understand, that I can do what I cannot do. I explain it by the fact that music acts like yawning, like laughter: I am not sleepy, but I yawn when I see someone yawning; there is nothing for me to laugh at, but I laugh when I hear people laughing.

"Music carries me immediately and directly into the mental condition in which the man was who composed it. My soul merges with his and together with him I pass from one condition into another, but why this happens I don't know. You see, he who wrote, let us say, the Kreutzer Sonata—Beethoven—knows of course why he was in that condition; that condition caused him to do certain actions and therefore that condition had a meaning for him, but for me—none at all. That is why music only agitates and doesn't lead to a conclusion. Well, when a military march is played the soldiers march to the music and the music has achieved its object. A dance is played, I dance and the music has achieved its object. Mass has been sung, I receive Communion, and that music too has reached a conclusion. Otherwise it is only agitating, and what ought to be done in that agitation is lacking. That is why music sometimes acts so dreadfully, so terribly. In China, music is a State affair. And that is as it should be. How can one allow anyone who pleases to hypnotize another, or many others, and do what he likes with them? And especially that this hypnotist should be the first immoral man who turns up?

"It is a terrible instrument in the hands of any chance user! Take that Kreutzer Sonata, for instance, how can that first presto be played in a drawing-room among ladies in low-necked dresses? To hear that played, to clap a little, and then to eat ices and talk of the latest scandal? Such things should only be played on certain important significant occasions, and then only when certain actions answering to such music are wanted; play it then and do what the music has moved you to. Otherwise an awakening of energy and feeling unsuited both to the time and the place, to which no outlet is given, cannot but act harmfully. At any rate that piece had a terrible effect

on me; it was as if quite new feelings, new possibilities, of which I had till then been unaware, had been revealed to me. That's how it is: not at all as I used to think and live, but that way, something seemed to say within me. What this new thing was that had been revealed to me I could not explain to myself, but the consciousness of this new condition was very joyous. All those same people, including my wife and him, appeared in a new light."[74]

There are only seven notes, but music is endless, just as endless are the responses born among the listeners. The more complex the music, the deeper it can move us, the more complicated the scale of emotions reflected within us, to which we gain access thanks to the music. What I do with them—do I project them upon the external (including the music itself) or do I own them, and, in that way, learn something about myself?—that is my choice. That is why I think that listening to complicated pieces of music can be a useful exercise in training the ability to be present. To be present, among other things, for our own reactions. I need to develop my ability to respond, to resonate. To become a kind of tuning fork. In resonating I can hear myself as well, and I can experience my "sounding" not as an obstacle but as a tool in building relationships. Including with myself. Or—let me be more precise—with myself first and foremost. The more obstacles we carry, obstacles that separate us within ourselves, the harder it is for us to hear the surrounding and the more we are locked within our own boundaries and limitations. But it is important for us to be open, because the field of therapeutic relationships is talking to us in the language of resonance.

That is precisely why we learn to make this process a conscious one, why we develop and cultivate within ourselves the capacity for resonance. It can be experienced physically as bodily sensations—for example, vibration, heaviness or pressure; it can be expressed in images, feelings, thoughts, or in the shape of a vague unclear emotion. Akin to Gendlin's *felt sense*. In order to train our capacity for resonance we need to single out something in our experience that at this moment in time attracts the most attention. It can be some kind of tension or

---

[74] Tolstoy, L., trans. by Louise and Aylmer Maude, *The Kreutzer Sonata*, web edition by Tolstoy Library OnLine

heaviness, or vague, unclear sensation, feeling, or image. In order to experience them more precisely you can try to intensify your feelings. The most important thing is not to rush, but simply to observe what happens in the meantime. And simultaneously to ask yourself, how can what you are experiencing be connected to the events in your life. While you are doing this, try to broaden your perspective to include not only today, but also your entire personal history. Which moments in your life, which days or hours or moments resonate in you right now? Try to grasp to what exactly, at this point in time, does your soul resonate.

Risk and the Unknown

*If I cut myself deeply, I will get hurt, but if at
the same time I believe that it shouldn't have
happened, I will suffer.*

Ragnvald Kvalsund is a bright, funny person, a talented psychologist, a great musician. I don't know anyone else who plays guitar as well. We have met many times, at conferences in Norway, in the United States, in Russia. Ragnvald was born and grew up in a small fishing village in Norway. His destiny seemed predetermined: all the boys who grew up in the village became fishermen. It was a real, manly profession, a typical male destiny in those parts. That was why, after graduating high school, Ragnvald, without thinking twice, went to work as a sailor on a fishing boat. But his very first sail turned out to be his last: as soon as the ship left the harbor he became seasick, and by the time he stepped ashore he was half-dead. There was absolutely no way he could make a career as a fisherman. Saddened by this, the family decided to send Ragnvald to a relative who was a farmer. After all, he had to do something in life—if he couldn't make it here, maybe he could be of use someplace else, even if farming was clearly not as good.

But in this new place an unpleasant surprise awaited Ragnvald as well. As soon as the gardens and fields began to bloom in spring, he developed such powerful allergies that he had to go first to the hospital and then home, to his fishing village. The family was not prepared for such a turn of events. Absolutely no one could have foreseen that Ragnvald would grow up to be such a useless young man! And because, *apparently*, he was no good for anything else, he was sent to the city to study. In the city, Ragnvald graduated from the university. He got a PhD. He became a professor… But the side of the family that lives in the fishing village still considers him to be a ne'er-do-well because he could not learn a real, manly skill, did not meet their expectations.

Once, after a seminar in Norway, Ragnvald and I watched a documentary about the American philosopher and spiritual teacher Ram Dass. The movie was about the courage with which this man dealt with the severe consequences of a stroke. There is a part in the movie in which Ram Dass meets a young woman, who turns to him for advice after her fiancé dies in a car accident. She bemoans her fate, tells Ram Dass about her broken love, her ruined life expectations, shares her pain and bitterness. He responds with compassion and tears in his eyes, "He has ruined all your plans." It is a very strong response, but is very truthful. Much of the suffering happens because our plans, our expectations, do not come to be.

Our expectations—a preliminary knowledge—is how we think *things ought to be*. But if there exist, in our life, moments of truth, then they occur when we truly become open to the unknown, when we undertake an experience at our own risk. At such moments we do not feel any support because we face the unknowable. Unknowable in the sense that we cannot know it *in advance*, because we have not yet experienced it, have not lived through it, it has not yet developed inside us: it is not yet our knowledge. The only thing that belongs to me is that which I have nurtured in myself, acquired through my own experience, through my own trials of life. It is my only way to reality. Reality is different from expectations. Hence the risk, and the fear— we don't know how everything will turn out.

Kierkegaard called preliminary knowledge *the sickness unto death*. An encounter with life comes through the unknown, the uncertainty, the fog of not knowing, darkness. Thence: unavoidable risk. But it is only through such risk that changes can take place in life, only through our own lack of understanding, through our own Shadow.

Since we're on the subject of Shadow, fear, and the unknown, it is high time we remember death. The philosopher Lev Shestov cites an old fable about how the angel of death, who descends upon a person to separate the person's body from the soul, is entirely covered in eyes. Why, wonders Shestov, does this angel need so many eyes—this angel who sees everything in heaven and who has nothing to look at on earth? Maybe these eyes are not for him. Sometimes it happens that the angel of death shows up to get the soul and realizes that he has come too early, that the time for this person has not yet come. On such occasions, before leaving, the angel stealthily takes a pair of eyes out of the multitude, and slips them to this person. In such a way this person receives new vision from darkness, and he begins to see something in addition to what everyone else can see, and in addition to what he can see with his own two old eyes. And then there begins a battle between the two visions, two ways of seeing. But this is a "fight unto life." There is a gift in this difference of potentials. If we were to develop the metaphor about the second, different vision, we could say that we need to develop within ourselves the capacity for such *consciously different seeing*. Maybe we can consider it a kind of professional practice.

I found an example of such ability to see differently in the work of the Israeli writer Meir Shalev. He has an episode in which a boy named Zayde asks his mother to buy him a wristwatch. This is what she tells him:

> *"You don't need a watch, Zayde. See how many watches there are in the world."*
>
> *She showed me the shadow of the eucalyptus that said nine in the morning with its size, its direction, and its chill, the little red leaves of the pomegranate that said mid-March, the tooth that wriggled in my mouth and said six years, and the small wrinkle in the corners of her eyes that capered and said forty.*
>
> *"You see, Zayde, this way you're inside time. If they bought you a watch, you'd only be next to it."*[75]

What does psychotherapy have to do with it? A similar idea works in therapy: if we are to orient toward the external techniques (it doesn't matter what kind of techniques—all of them are "preliminary

---

[75] Shalev, M., *The Loves of Judith*, Schocken, 2012, pp. 100-101

knowledge") then we always will remain somewhere *next to* relationships, somewhere to the side of them, but not *inside* the relationships. If we see another person as a problem that we must solve, then this other person will forever remain for us an obstacle. An obstacle to something. To a lunch break or to professional success— it doesn't matter, still: an obstacle. That is to say, the client will be separated by our own limitations. But if we manage in our encounter with the Other to be open to the unknown, the secret, then we will discover ourselves immersed in it, captivated by it. And this opens up a completely different perspective, a completely different way of seeing. New eyes. Otherwise, instead of the open space of therapeutic relationships, we risk finding ourselves in the cramped cubicle of a taxidermist where the living human feelings of the Other turn into a dead animal stuffed with someone else's (and alien) context. And that is amoral.

The Perception of Inner Beauty

Contemporary culture actively promotes an image of a person geared toward achievement: it is necessary to strive upward, to be effective, to match up to high expectations, to achieve success, to obtain, to use, to travel, to go to the gym. Beautiful life! It is prestigious. In French, *prestige* means "glamour, dazzling influence." Curiously, the word originates in late Latin *praestigium*, which means "illusion," from Latin *praestigiae*, "conjuring tricks."

A dear friend once was invited to the house of a wealthy couple who tended toward spiritual practices. The house was beautifully furnished, and there were many expensive objects. The owner of the house showed my friend a special room for meditation and said that it was built "to fit a carpet." Asked what that meant, the owner explained: "We bought a very beautiful carpet and decided to build an addition to the house to fit it, so we could meditate there. We want everything in our meditation room to be beautiful."

Some people believe that the sensation of beauty comes to them from beautiful objects, so that if there is not enough beauty surrounding them, then there is no sensation of beauty. Moreover, "beautiful" objects inevitably come accompanied by "non-beautiful" objects, which interfere in our ability to sense beauty. For example, an ugly rotting stump on the lawn ruins our impression of the beautiful music we hear, or the smell of petrol from the street interferes with our ability to enjoy the beauty of a rose bush. Proust calls such people "spiritual materialists," and Mamardashvili writes: "Beauty is contained not in a beautiful object but in a transformation, a gradient of this transformation. And therefore the smell of petrol cannot become an interference. A soul that is capable of transformation, or a generous soul, can transform even the petrol around itself because the source of moral and spiritual shift is not in the environment…Petrol is not a rose, of course, but beauty does not originate in a rose and it does not originate in petrol…The personal source is elsewhere. It is in the point of equilibrium. And there it does not depend on petrol, or on a rose. What I experience when I am surrounded by petrol fumes and what I experience when I look upon a rose must be equidistant from a certain point—a point of equilibrium, a singular point. And then throughout this space there will occur a fullness of existence. The man is alive! But to wait until the entire environment consists of just social relations, of beautiful objects…is a futile task."[76]

Mamardashvili writes about the point of equilibrium as of a place within our soul "where we are all equal, all 'in the nude,' without qualities. All qualities are taken off. The only thing that matters is the level or gradient of transformation that originates in this point. Depending on the extent to which you are invested in an emotion, to which you have engaged in it at your own risk. A state can be high or low: I can be reading a genius book or looking at a flower. But you have to be present in this point yourself, you have to invest…And if we invest ourselves, the world becomes pierced by us, that which happens to us depends on our investment."

The greatest Greek philosophers ascend to the highest realm of being not merely through thinking but also through mystical experience. They characterize it as a sphere of absolute beauty. Plato uses the famous cave allegory, which is considered to be the cornerstone of his teaching, and in which he depicts shackled people who sit inside the cave with their backs to the source of light, looking at the wall and seeing only the shadows of the things that are being carried behind their backs, between them and the source of light. In this myth, Plato talks about a sensuous world inhabited by people who

---

[76] Mamardashvili, M., *Psikhologicheskaya topologiya puti*, Izdatel'stvo Russkogo Khristianskogo Gumanitarnogo Instituta, 1997

believe that they are acquiring knowledge about the world, while in truth they are only observing its shadows, not reality.

> *[W]hen any of them is liberated and compelled suddenly to stand up and turn his neck round and walk and look towards the light, he will suffer sharp pains; the glare will distress him, and he will be unable to see the realities of which in his former state he had seen the shadows…*
>
> *He will require to grow accustomed to the sight of the upper world. And first he will see the shadows best, next the reflections of men and other objects in the water, and then the objects themselves; then he will gaze upon the light of the moon and the stars and the spangled heaven; and he will see the sky and the stars by night better than the sun or the light of the sun by day…*
>
> *And when he remembered his old habitation, and the wisdom of the den and his fellow-prisoners, do you not suppose that he would felicitate himself on the change, and pity them?…*
>
> *And if they were in the habit of conferring honours among themselves on those who were quickest to observe the passing shadows and to remark which of them went before, and which followed after, and which were together; and who were therefore best able to draw conclusions as to the future, do you think that he would care for such honours and glories, or envy the possessors of them?…*
>
> *Imagine once more…such a one coming suddenly out of the sun to be replaced in his old situation; would he not be certain to have his eyes full of darkness?…*
>
> *And if there were a contest, and he had to compete in measuring the shadows with the prisoners who had never moved out of the den, while his sight was still weak, and before his eyes had become steady (and the time which would be needed to acquire this new habit of sight might be very considerable) would he not be ridiculous? Men would say of him that up he went and down he came without his eyes; and that it was better not even to think of ascending; and if any one tried to loose another and lead him up to the light, let them only catch the offender, and they would put him to death….*
>
> *[Y]ou will not misapprehend me if you interpret the journey upwards to be the ascent of the soul into the intellectual world…my opinion is that in*

> *the world of knowledge the idea of good appears last of all, and is seen only with an effort; and, when seen, is also inferred to be the universal author of all things beautiful and right, parent of light and of the lord of light in this visible world, and the immediate source of reason and truth in the intellectual; and that this is the power upon which he who would act rationally, either in public or private life must have his eye fixed.*[77]

This fable compares the idea of goodness to the sun, and the ability to discern it is described as the source of the beautiful and right. The idea of goodness is compared to beauty. It is precisely in the idea of goodness, according to Plato, that there lies the cause of right and beautiful. The ability to contemplate true beauty, to discern it, leads to the contemplation of goodness. The path to such contemplation requires internal work, internal transformation.

To make this internal ascent, as Plato says in *The Republic*, one needs to start with the easiest.

The windows of our apartment face a courtyard. It is a typical old St. Petersburg courtyard. We live on the top floor and our windows face some rooftops and the sky. Opposite our windows, crows promenade on the rooftops. If you lie in bed you can look at the sky, nothing obstructs it. A few years ago, my elder daughter came to visit us after a few years of absence and could not help painting a triptych, the view of the roofs across the yard from our windows. Then she turned this painting into an avatar for her email. Recently an old friend stopped by. He came up to the window, looked at the roof and the wall across the yard and said, "This building is in such a terrible condition, its plaster is peeling." I was surprised, because I had always thought the building rather picturesque. "Mold can take root in it," my friend explained. It occurred to me that what we see depends on the place in our soul from which we look at the world, on the context that is invisibly present in our seeing. And I remembered Kant's saying, "The *beautiful* is that which, apart from a concept, pleases universally," which is to say, the beauty of a butterfly's wings is seen in no relation to these wings' ability to lift and carry weight.

---

[77] Plato, *The Republic, Book VII*

The books of the psychotherapist and poet Viktor Kagan are read by specialists and by people unrelated to this profession alike. Since the early 1990s, Viktor has been among the people who have nurtured Harmony. A PhD and the author of many books on psychiatry and psychotherapy, Viktor Kagan is one of the brightest Russian psychotherapists. Such was his fate that, in the late 1990s, he moved to the United States, and now he lives and works there. And writes poetry. And takes photographs, for pleasure. Kagan writes:

> *It happens in life that suddenly you look up at a person amid the bustle and noise—and by some miracle everything, except for that person, retreats somewhere into the background, loses focus, becomes unimportant. Let's say, if you have ever fallen in love—not at first sight, at God knows which, having known the person for a long time, but suddenly you were illuminated by a completely different vision of him or her, and there opened for you Something that until that moment had been secret, turning him or her from someone into the center of creation. Or—this is more mundane, psychologists will understand me—the way it happens during a psychotherapy session, when you are with a client and you see him or her in such a light and with such qualities in which and with which you will not see him or her outside of the session. Herein lies the difference of the art of directed or studio photography, which creates beauty and allows a person to be in it, and to become embodied into a fixed memory of his or her magical transformation. Not elevating the mundane to the level of the beautiful, but a revelation of beauty (not the beauty of gloss but the beauty of living expression) in the mundane—such is the idea that is partly, of course, connected to photographic unprofessionalism.*[78]

I think that this ability to have a revelation, to see the beauty of the Other and to reflect it, is mainly connected to therapeutic professionalism. Seeing inner beauty is akin to experiencing *felt sense*. I think many of my colleagues are familiar with this sudden revelation of the singularity of the person sitting in front of you, as if a shroud falls and a new vision opens, and you are surprised to see inside of yourself a new, attuned perception of his or her uniqueness and beauty.

---

[78] Kagan, V., http://vekagan.livejournal.com/496954.html, 2011

Of course the ability to see beauty is not monopolized by psychologists and is not limited to psychotherapy. Moreover, the revelation of beauty can take place under what may seem to be the least conducive circumstances. For example, in the labor camps of Stalin's Gulag:

> *"Abandon hope all ye who enter here…"*
> *And yet: behold the miracle of a ripe tree bud,*
> *the stubborn growth inside the crusty taiga,*
> *and you will say: "There's a way out of here."*[79]
>   *S. Bondarin*

Seeing beauty gives birth to the miracle of a new way of seeing life, it unfolds the situation from a completely different perspective, opens a new perspective, leads to spiritual enlightenment, and fills with strength and humanity under difficult, inhumane conditions.

The Turkish writer Orhan Pamuk speaks about the ability to see beauty where it is invisible to an accustomed eye when he points out that the inimitable beauty of Istanbul was discovered by Europeans— outsiders, strangers to that land and culture. To the locals the city always seemed poor, crumbling, shrouded in chagrin and melancholy. "Because he saw the city like an *Istanbullu* but painted it like a clear-eyed Westerner, Melling's Istanbul is not only a city graced by hills, mosques, and places that we recognize, it is a place of sublime beauty."[80] One has to be a stranger, Pamuk believes, in order to enjoy the beauty of the poor quarters, in order to perceive the amazingness, the magic and the uniqueness of a city that arises in your view. It is precisely the absence of bias that allows one to encounter the genuineness, to accept it as it is. Another European, the British writer and art historian John Ruskin, spoke of the picturesque beauty of Istanbul buildings that appeared hundreds of years after the buildings were constructed, when vines wove their braids around the walls and grass sprouted in the cracks. He pointed out that what made picturesque beauty different was its accidental nature. Paradoxically,

---

[79] *Poeziya uznikov GULAGa: Antologiya*, MFD-Materik, 2005, p. 642
[80] Pamuk, O., *Istanbul: Memories and the City*, Vintage, 2006, p. 75

beauty is to be found in the doomed. Such beauty cannot be fixed, it is always sudden, accidental.

But not all strangers are able to see such picturesque beauty, it is not enough to merely be a stranger. I know people who see in Istanbul a crumbling and impoverished city, even though they are strangers in it.

Why does this happen? What prevents us from seeing beauty in the crumbling and the impoverished? Why does peeling plaster cause concern that "mold can take root in it," why does it block the view of the picturesque beauty of a building?

In order to answer these questions we may need to turn to the ancient Greek concepts of *chaos* and *cosmos* and their interaction.

The concept of *chaos* takes its name from the ancient Greek idea of the original state of the world as a yawning chasm out of which the first gods emerged. Later, chaos became endowed with the meanings of disorder, confusion, disorganized elements. Chaos is unsafe. You don't know what to expect from it. Its whole essence lies in this unrealized potential. When we encounter chaos we encounter the uncertain, the unsettled. The uncertain makes us feel tense. A cracked wall with peeling plaster has an air of anxiety. The wall is falling apart. Nothing lasts forever. Including myself. An unpleasant thought.

One wants to bring everything to order almost as a reflex. How to avoid seeing all this? One wants a cosmetic repair that would conceal the truth of the naked brick, remove from sight the unpleasantness of the collapsing framework. It is believed that the word *cosmetics* is derived from the idea of *cosmos*: "order." The philosopher Pythagoras is believed to have been the first to use the word *cosmos* to describe the beauty and deep order of the universe, its harmony and the proportionality of its components. After Pythagoras, Greek philosophers used the word *cosmos* to represent a system or an organism infused with logic as opposed to a random conglomeration of creatures and phenomena. Thanks to Pythagoras, the world stopped looking like *chaos* and began to look like *cosmos*. In this manner, *cosmos* was overcoming *chaos* because it was exceeding it.

That may be the solution: to keep *cosmos* in mind.

Maybe then we will be able to consciously allow ourselves to encounter our experience without trying to change it, to come into contact with the "truth" of our experience, regardless of how it is expressed—even if our experience is unclear to us, even if it is connected to pain, even if it is uncomfortable and frightening. Of course this will require courage on our part because often experience challenges our stereotypes. But, after a while, we will discover that when we are prepared to accept our experience the way it is, something new and useful emerges within us, and in the end we feel more wholesome. We will discover that the sensation of chaos is temporary and that it is replaced with a sensation of deep order. "The chaos ... brings us more than we could ever imagine when we are able to stay with it and live into the deep order/meaning that emerges from it...From this experience of deep order, in turn, arises new understanding. Our minds now recognize and can hold the pattern and learning that have arisen from the sheer living of the experience and the bearing of the chaos until meaning emerged. We can now think and reflect on how this learning can be applied in our life."[81]

From this sensation of deep order, in turn, there will arise a new understanding, a new way of seeing the beauty of the cosmos. No cosmetics will get us there. Despite its pleasant name and its noble origins, cosmetics turns out to be an obliging handmaiden of chaos, a handmaiden that trembles before it and masks it.

We need chaos. We must be in contact with it.

From chaos we need to learn cosmos.

But how?

---

[81]Yeomans, T., *Living Experience as Spiritual Practice*, Occasional Note No. 8, 2003

An Ethical Paradox

Let me start by telling you what stunned me once and continues to stun me each time I encounter Rembrandt: his painting of Abraham sacrificing Isaac. Whenever I visit the Hermitage, I study this painting, and I sense a connection with the mystery enshrouded within it. The mystery of Abraham and Isaac, the mystery of father-son relationships, and, the way I see it, the mystery of Man… Like many others I study the painting, turn to the quotes from the Holy Bible, to the works of theologians and philosophers, trying to discover the clue. And, like many others, I rely on the spiritual response these sources elicit when characters of religious plots seem to come alive in the mind…

> *"On the third day Abraham lifted up his eyes, and saw the place from a distance" (Gen. 22:4). What did he see? He saw a pillar of fire standing from the earth to the heavens. He said to Isaac his son, "My son, do you see anything on one of these mountains?" He said to him, "Yes, I see a pillar of fire standing from the earth to the heavens." He said to Ishmael and Eliezer, "Do you see anything on one of these mountains?" "No." He considered them asses and said to them, "Remain here with the ass."*[82]

I look at the painting and recall that in the Scriptures it says that "the two of them went on together" up the mountain to perform the sacrifice (Gen. 22:6). These words insist thrice, as if underscoring, on purpose, that there were two of them ascending the mountain. Why, then, does Genesis 22:19 say that only "Abraham returned to his servants"—not "Abraham and Isaac," but Abraham alone? What

---

[82] Hauser, A., Watson, D., *A History of Biblical Interpretation, Vol. 2,* Wm. B. Eerdmans Publishing Co., 2009, p. 120-121

happened to Isaac up there, on the mountain, *after* the Angel had stopped the hand that had been prepared to slaughter him? Why did he not descend the mountain together with his father? I do not see his face in the painting. I am trying to imagine… I bring my friends to this painting, in the hope for a clue in their explanations and reactions, and many times I hear: "I don't understand why God would order Abraham to do this. How could he be so cruel?!"

This also was what I heard from my Norwegian friend, the wonderful Norwegian psychotherapist Nils Grendstad, when I brought him to the Hermitage one time. Nils told me that when he was a child his father had taught him to weed carrots. He had explained to Nils that he had to concentrate on carrot leaves and weed everything else, otherwise he was running the risk of weeding the carrots along with everything else. "You have to focus on the good," Assagioli would tell him later, "the bad will take care of itself." Like many Norwegians, Nils was religious. His kindness stemmed from the kindness of God.

I am not a theologian, I am a psychotherapist, a doctor and a psychologist, and this has an impact on the way I see human mysteries. In the painting, I see the almost deranged face of an elder—yellowish-gray, the deadest object. Abraham's left hand tilts back Isaac's head, covering his face. So that the boy doesn't see? So that he himself doesn't see? The knife is falling from Abraham's right hand, which is held back by the Angel; the angel's hand is raised above Abraham's head as if to slap him. The painting arrests an instant. The knife is still falling, its blade still points at Isaac's throat. Isaac seems impotent, only his left leg is bent with tension, only this leg betrays some tension in his body, some resistance. The hands of Abraham and the hands of the angel. We don't see Isaac's hands—his father has bound them behind his back. And yet, among all the characters in this painting, it is precisely Abraham who causes the viewers to experience the most emotions—because he is the one who has to sacrifice, he is the one who has to make the hard decision…Paradoxically, Isaac, whom Rembrandt has disrobed, denuded, and placed the closest to the viewer, seems to vanish into the background, disappear from view, because he does not appear at a crossroads; his role is the role of a sacrificial sheep, an impotent victim. The painting doesn't show his face—the father's hand conceals, defaces, separates Isaac's emotions from the viewer.

Only Abraham returned to his servants…

Again and again, the mystery of Isaac remains unseen. What happened to the beloved child of the "knight of faith?" He was not killed on the altar, but he left it a changed man. What did he look like? What did Isaac carry away from this trial, what had it taught him? He did not walk down the mountain with his father.

Only Abraham returned to his servants…

Of course it is wrong to interpret the biblical fable literally. It is directed at the heart of the reader, at the spot where, in Novalis's words, internal and external worlds collide, and one can only comprehend it by looking inward. It is impossible to understand it by looking at it from any place other than one's own soul. The potential of the fable, its strength, are contained in the fact that it addresses the internal experience of everyone who comes into contact with it, which is precisely why, for centuries, it has been attracting and resonating among people from a multitude of cultures. Any attempts to understand it literally are useless. All answers to the questions must be sought within ourselves. The painting or the text can only direct the search, offer beacons.

"Let us try for a moment to look into Abraham's soul when he was commanded to sacrifice his only son," writes Jung. "Quite apart from the compassion he felt for his child, would not a father in such a position feel himself as the victim, and feel that he was plunging the knife into his own breast? *He would be at the same time the sacrificer and the sacrificed* [my italics—A.B.]."[83] It is difficult to entirely agree with this: there is an enormous difference between sacrificing something, even something that is the most dear, and sacrificing oneself. Besides, it is difficult to imagine "a father in such a position," although it is quite possible to imagine a father killing his own son, and history knows of many such crimes. Some of them have become the subjects of

---

[83] Clasby, N., *God, the Bible, and Human Consciousness*, Palgrave Macmillan, 2008, p. 61

paintings, inspired creativity, so to speak. In Russian art we have the examples of Ivan the Terrible and Peter the Great. Both of them, undoubtedly, suffered from their actions. But when one stands before Ilya Repin's painting "Ivan the Terrible killing his son" one feels a completely different set of emotions. Here before us is a crime, the horror of irrevocability of the action, and not a sacrifice. A crime has motives, or else it can be explained by an affect, for example, or some kind of personal rationale. In Friedrich Gorenstein's play *Infanticide*, Peter the Great explains his decision by saying, "I sacrifice my son to the superior service of the state."[84] There is a "sacrifice," but there also is an explanation: a political advantage.

It is impossible to *explain*, to *understand* the sacrifice of Isaac by Abraham. Ivan the Terrible committed murder out of rage, Peter the Great out of political calculation. Abraham walked up Mount Moriah full of love for his son. Full of faith. But faith in what? Faith—but not certainty, says Kierkegaard, "the absurdity of faith." Kierkegaard tried to understand Abraham—the "knight of faith"—in his relationship with God. But not Isaac.

Abraham stood alone before God, and there was no one near him who could have shared his lot. There was no one and there could not have been anyone because no one else had the kind of relationship with God that Abraham had. No one else had the kind of commitment to God. He was alone, this was the highest form of solitude—solitude before God.

Nor did Isaac see Abraham's God.

From the religious point of view, Abraham wanted to sacrifice Isaac for God; from the ethical point of view, he was plotting an infanticide. Kierkegaard saw the essence of this monstrous paradox of Abraham's life as a contradiction between the ethical and the religious, between the "general" and the "singular." In trying to understand Abraham, Kierkegaard used as a starting point the idea that it is the task of ethics to demonstrate which answer to the question of what to do is correct *in general*, because ethically there is a *general* that is mandatory for everyone. Ethics applies to everyone in the same measure; from the

---

[84] Gorenstein, F., *Tri pyesy*, Word, 1988

point of view of ethics, every father is linked to his child by the most sacred, sublime obligation—that is a general rule that applies to all fathers in regards to their children.

From the point of view of ethics, the singular is lesser than the general, is contained within the general and therefore is subject to the general. From the point of view of ethics, the attitude of Abraham toward Isaac must be contained entirely in the notion that a father must love his son. While the religious is *singular*, because it presupposes a relationship between a singular person and God. Such relationships are singular and absolute because they presuppose a relationship between a single human and the absolute.[85]

Kierkegaard talks about the existence of an absolute relationship toward God, juxtaposing the absolute religious and the relative ethical. Abraham has no answer to the question "Why?" other than that it is a test, a temptation he has withstood for God and for himself. Neither of these definitions relates to the other in the commonly accepted language. According to this language, when a person acts in a way that goes against the *generally accepted*, such a person is described as having done this for himself, and not for God. Meanwhile, the paradox of faith lacks the connecting link—it lacks the *general*. On the one hand, it represents the highest form of egoism (committing a horrible crime in the name of oneself); on the other, absolute selflessness: committing it in the name of God.

A relationship with God, in Kierkegaard's mind, erases commonly accepted norms. In such a relationship "[e]ither the individual becomes a knight of faith by assuming the burden of the paradox, or he never becomes one. In these regions partnership is unthinkable. Every more precise explication of what is to be understood by Isaac the individual can give only to himself. And even if one were able, generally speaking, to define ever so precisely what should be intended by Isaac (which moreover would be the most ludicrous self-contradiction, i.e. that the particular individual who definitely stands outside the universal is subsumed under universal categories precisely when he has to act as the individual who stands outside the universal), the individual

---

[85] Buber, M., *Two Types of Faith*, Macmillian, 1951, p. 22

nevertheless will never be able to assure himself by the aid of others that this application is appropriate, but he can do so only by himself as the individual."[86]

But we are interested in Isaac—it's time to think about him. Yet, our hearts are troubled by these words: "*what* is to be understood by Isaac" and "*what* should be *intended* by Isaac" [my italics—A.B.]. The paradox Abraham took upon himself has turned Isaac from a *beloved only son* into a "*what*," a thing, a *tool* of Abraham's relationships with God; and Isaac has turned from the *singular* into the *general*. His singularity was somehow quietly removed. The relationship between a father and his only, beloved son, turned from *I-Thou* into *I-It*.

We do not see Isaac's face in the painting. Maybe he no longer has a face, as if he is nobody? The son of the knight of faith!

Later he himself will become blind and will be unable to tell his sons from one another.

Questions multiply and remain unsolved. What if the voice that had demanded that Abraham sacrifice his son had not belonged to God at all?

It is possible that the story of Abraham and Isaac reflects an eternally unresolvable human drama. It is impossible to understand them together, at the same time. One of them always will remain misunderstood. The world does not recover. Joseph Brodsky was right when he said, in his Nobel acceptance speech, that it is probably too late to save the world but "for the individual man there always remains a chance." That is precisely what therapy does—it helps one man. Therein lies its paradox.

Human suffering is always singular. If there are three sick people in a hospital ward, it is absurd to suggest that had there only been one, there would have been three times less pain. C.S. Lewis[87] believes that the moment a person reaches the maximum level of suffering, the level of suffering in the universe also reaches its peak—that suffering cannot be added to suffering, that it is singular, and that its singular is greater than the general, because it contains the general. That is why

---

[86] Kierkegaard, S., *Fear and Trembling*, Merchant Books, 2012, p. 53
[87] Lewis, C.S., *The Problem of Pain*, William Collins, 2012

psychotherapy is always singular. Therefore, it always presupposes a kind of transformation of the ethical, an *ethical paradox*.

The task of ethics is to demonstrate what is good and what is evil. Ethics is *general*, ethics responds to the question what is *generally* good and what is *generally* right, *applicable to one and all*. Ethics considers everyone equally. For example, from the point of view of ethics, every parent is connected to his or her child with the most sacred obligation—that is the general rule that applies to all parents as they relate to their children. The same is true for the attitude of children toward their parents. Children *in general* toward parents *in general*. And if some parent/child displays toward his or her child/parent rudeness, violence, we consider that to be evil. If such evil takes place right next to us, then everything within us protests, we are ready to interfere in order to stop the violence: *the moral law* within us speaks.

In a therapeutic situation, the natural ethical, moral reaction is transformed and replaced with *empathic response*. One can say that in a therapeutic situation, the ethical *I-He, I-She, I-It* is transformed into the ethical *I-Thou*.

> *I remember once, when I was a young man, I was walking home and thinking that if I looked up and saw that the windows of the apartment were dark, that would be a sign, I would know that they have died. God, if you do exist, please make it so that my parents get into an accident, that they are killed in a car crash, that they are run over by a car, that a train tears them to shreds… Something! I beg you, God, if you do exist, please make it so! If I look up and see that the windows of the apartments are dark I will know that they have died. And then I turn the corner and I see: light in the windows!... And I realize that there is no God, otherwise He would have heard me!*[88]

What a horrific confession! But listen to the trembling voice, look into the eyes filled with tears, hear the rage and pain expressed for the first time ever by a forty-year-old man, sense the fear he feels as he connects with the painful memories, and you will understand the

---

[88] Badkhen, A., Rodina, A., *Terapevticheskoe prostranstvo: Masterstvo prikhologicheskogo konsul'tirovaniya*, Evropeiskii Dom, 2002, p. 52

meaning of this moment of supreme openness, earnestness, and defenselessness. It is possible that now, because of the therapist's ability to be present and to accept, for the first time in his life this person has a way to unravel the wounding details of his childhood. The moral law that under different circumstances could provoke an ethical *judgment* becomes, in therapeutic relationships, an empathic *response*. The rule of ethics is replaced by compassion.

The human need for compassion (com-passion) is the need for presence. Steven Levine describes the nature of compassion this way, "When your fear touches someone's pain it becomes pity; when your love touches someone's pain, it becomes compassion."[89] In order to be present for the other you have to clearly see your own boundaries and learn to observe yourself. If you want to turn to the soul of the other, you must, first and foremost, be in contact with your own soul.

Here it seems appropriate to mention another important principle pointed out by Carl Rogers (1961): "One way of putting this which may seem strange to you is that if I can form a helping relationship to myself—if I can be sensitively aware of and acceptant toward my own feelings—then the likelihood is great that I can form a helping relationship toward another."[90] In other words, if I am able to be present to what I am experiencing at this moment, abstaining from reactions and not resorting to different ways of defensiveness, then it is very likely that I will be able to create the conditions that will allow my client to meet himself or herself.

---

[89] Sogyal Rinpoche, *The Tibetan Book of Living and Dying*, Harper, 1992, p. 200
[90] Rogers, C., *On Becoming a Person: A Therapist's View of Psychotherapy*, Houghton Mifflin, 1961, p. 51

Therapeutic Acceptance

A true meeting requires an internal movement toward something, a kind of a reaching out, and we are not always capable of it. Such an intense connection, such orientation toward the Other, such openness, reaching out to the Other must *happen* each time—it cannot to be organized or established once and for all. It was not without reason that Buber tried to convey the temporary and unstable nature of this phenomenon, underscoring frequently its fleetingness, its near-ineffableness: "there are only moments;"[91] "in a receptive hour of my personal life;"[92] "this time of day."[93]

"Let us imagine that this is one of the hours which succeeded in bursting asunder the seven iron bands about our heart,"[94] he wrote, "only then, true to the moment, do we experience a life that is something other than a sum of moments. We respond to the moment but at the same time we respond on its behalf, we answer for it. A newly-created concrete reality has been laid into our arms; we answer for it. A dog has looked at you, you answer for its glance, a child has clutched your hand, you answer for its touch, a host of men moves about you, you answer for their need."[95]

A few years ago I involuntarily witnessed the following dialogue. I am quoting it here almost verbatim. It took place on a river beach, on a July evening. It had been a warm, sunny day, but by evening some clouds had begun to gather in the sky, and it was clearly going to rain.

---

[91] Buber, M., *Between Man and Man*, Routledge, 2002, p. 12

[92] Ibid, p. 11

[93] Ibid, p. 16

[94] Buber, M., *Between Man and Man*, Routledge, 2002, p. 4

[95] Ibid, p. 20

He, in swimming trunks, approaches the river. She, in slacks, t-shirt and a cardigan draped over her shoulders.

He *[wades into the water]*: The water is so cold!

She: Then get out.

[He wades knee-deep, obviously preparing to go for a swim.]

He: My ear hurts. I am about to catch cold.

She: Then get out immediately!

He: There's probably a lot of fish here. [Dives in.]

She: I feel cold just looking at you.

He *[emerges]*: I should get a dragnet from grandpa and go fishing.

[At this moment, lightning flashes in the sky, thunder can be heard.]

She: Get out quick. It's going to rain now.

He: Lightning is just two clouds that ran into each other. It doesn't have to rain.

[That very moment it begins to rain.]

She: There are already some drops.

He: Do you know what a dragnet is? It's a net and two sticks…

On the one hand, the participants are in constant contact; on the other, the contact between them is obviously broken and this creates the sensation that what is taking place is absurd. But the dialogue begins to sound entirely different, it obtains a new meaning, if we learn of the exchange between them that had taken place earlier, as they approached the river. In fact, this very exchange sets the tone for the conversation:

He: The dacha is great. We should help grandma pick berries.

She: I can't stand your grandma! And I don't like coming to the dacha, either.

A part of their mental energy remains shackled to these words, although they do not return to them specifically. The epicenter of the conflict remains too close, and neither of them has yet had the opportunity to turn to it directly. The conversation by the river, which may seem absurd, is merely the tip of the iceberg; the main mass of feelings is hidden under the surface of the words they say and does not yet have an outlet. But it actually does express itself in the stubborn deafness. Dissociation can be resolved by living through the experience.

These questions may seem a kind of nitpicking, but our soul is contained in the minutia, the details, and therapists must practice recognizing their shades in themselves and in others. When we notice the differences, variety, multifacetedness in ourselves and in others, the level of our identification changes and our complexity emerges. Complexity is important and one shouldn't try to simplify it. On the contrary, we should support and accept it. The task of a therapist is precisely to allow the complexity to transpire. It is important to support seeing in perspective so that a multilayered image does not become flat. All of us—the clients, the therapists—have a choice: to ignore or to hide from complexity in ourselves or to acknowledge it and integrate it into our experience. The complexity of experience allows us to approach the whole, true existence instead of identifying with one of its aspects, one part, which stands out at the forefront at this particular moment, blocking the entire perspective (like the crumbs in my story). Experience is fluid and inconsistent; if we allow ourselves to see new details of experience emerge again and again, then we are able to enter into a relationship with it. Remember that to be an ally means to accept an experience without trying to change it. In a way, an accepting psychotherapist can be compared to an obstetrician: he or she makes sure that the birthing process develops naturally and receives the newborn. At the same time, no one has any doubt that the newborn baby belongs not to the obstetrician, but to the mother.

Recently I met with a client who came for a consultation from a different city. In her own city she went to a psychotherapist, the senior psychotherapist of her city, who listened to her and said: "You have anxiety-depressive disorder, I will prescribe some pills, you will take them, and in a few days you'll come back and see me again."

This did not happen in some back-of-beyond. This took place in a large, industrial Russian city with a population of one million. I dare suppose that such things happen in my country all the time. It all depends on whether a given specialist sees a person as an object of change (treatment, upbringing, etc.) or a subject of development. In the first case, there exist norms and rules, which I impose upon the Other. These norms and rules, which this other person has to abide, exist as if outside this person; it is as if they have arisen before any particular person ever appeared. Therefore, they represent a certain standard, a set of conditions for a person's existence, and if the person is not in compliance with these norms and rules, than this person's very existence is questionable. Adaptation, conformism, or compromise are the necessary conditions for such existence. But if one treats the Other as a subject of development, that takes us to a completely different position. In this case, we take on the role of a guide who supports the existence of the other. It is easy to see that in the first case we are closer to the external, and in the second—to the internal, essential aspect of existence.

If a psychotherapist limits himself or herself to prescribing pills, or "is satisfied to 'analyze' his or her patient, i.e., to bring to light unknown factors from the patient's microcosm, and to set to some conscious work the energies that have been transformed by such an emergence, and to apply to a conscious project the energies that have been transformed by this emergence—he may successfully accomplish some repairs...But he cannot absolve his true task, which is the regeneration of a stunted personal center."[96] In order to help recover the coherence between a person and the world, "the therapist, like the educator, must stand not only at his own pole of the bipolar relationship but also at the other pole, experiencing the effects of his own actions."[97] Buber unites in his thoughts a psychotherapist and an educator because in order to help realize the best potential in the student's nature an educator, a teacher must see in him or her not a simple sum of qualities, but must recognize the student as a whole and accept him or her in his or her wholeness.

At first glance, such thoughts seem simple and self-evident, but experience shows that even here mishaps often occur. For example, I recently witnessed a conversation between two female psychologists, who discussed the possibility of what they called "unconditional

---

[96] Buber, M., *I and Thou*, Charles Scribner's Sons, 1970
[97] Ibid.

acceptance," and the principals of humanistic psychology in the Russian school system in general:

"There are many children, each has his or her own wants, and it is difficult to approach each one—both to use the individual approach and to show empathy. What if I don't find any of them affable?" said one.

I was intrigued. To be affable means to leave a positive impression, to be likeable. So here, then, is the problem: what do I do if I don't like any of them, asks a specialist without so much as noticing the absurdity of such a question.

"For me, the idea of an unconditional acceptance is the most controversial, both from the point of view of education and from the point of view of the teaching process. It goes without question that to accept everything in the school process does not mean to shape a personality. To me it sounds this way because education is a process of prohibitions and a process of directing a child, shaping him. That's how it's been for me so far, and there is no alternative. If a child is running down the hallway and knocks others off their feet, I must stop him, I can't accept him unconditionally in his desire to express his energy," agreed her interlocutor.

"If we're talking about a child who comes from a family where everyone cusses and starts cussing in class, basically conveying what's happening at home, that's a different story. But then again, to which extent can a teacher hearing all this stop their own emotions that arise at that moment?" asked the first.

"I basically left the school system because of its rigidity," responded the other.

I am not inventing any of this and not adding anything. These were exactly the words they used. Their conversation continued along the same lines and, finally, from such a conversation, they drew the following conclusion: our Russian reality does not fit the ideas of humanistic psychology because our reality is too rigid—that is to say, the ideas of humanistic psychology are theoretically good, but they are not for us, or, if they are for us, they are not for us today. We, of course, are ready for them, but our school reality is not. Maybe at some point in the future the reality will become ready, at some point it will become softer, but right now it's not. And so there emerges the conclusion that "in the framework of the existing system…it is clear that humanistic pedagogy is, let's say, extremely problematic." That is to say that we, ourselves, are good, "humanistic," but the system and the conditions in which we live and work are letting us down. Had the conditions been different, then we also would have been different. This sounds so familiar! And the concept of acceptance that underlies it is so diluted.

If we want to understand this thoroughly, we must differentiate the semantic nuances of the concept of acceptance. In the common language "acceptance" is often used as a synonym of acquiescence or approval. In practical psychology and in therapy, the accent is on a different meaning of this concept. Here, acceptance is different from consent to ourselves or to the other, it is not the same as the approval of insufficiencies or the approval of weaknesses. To accept means to turn a calm and clear gaze upon both capabilities and limitations. Acceptance has to do with accepting *what really is*.

Acceptance is different from passivity and it is made possible by awareness. To accept someone means to see someone as a whole and to respond to him or her *as a whole*, and not to react to specific impulses or identifications. The same goes for acceptance of oneself. To accept myself means to be present to myself the way I am. It means to be aware of my own identification, to see clearly the internal contradictions and what limits me, as well as my possibilities, without at the same time pushing myself to any particular decision, but leaving for myself room for choosing. In a way, acceptance is a practice of disidentification and centeredness, it is a spiritual practice of self-discovery. Acceptance is an internal act. Acceptance requires us to see what is, and to manage with what we have and not to bemoan what we don't have. It is an internal act that relies on our maturity, which is to say on our ability to self-observe, to distinguish our own emotions; it demands of us to be able to move with a certain level of freedom inside our own internal landscape. We can sum up all of this with the famous saying by Carl Rogers, "The curious paradox is that when I accept myself just as I am, then I can change."

Psychotherapy is impossible without acknowledging the internal world. "I see you, and you see me. I experience you, and you experience me. I see your behaviour. You see my behaviour. But I do not and never have and never will see your *experience* of me. Just as you cannot 'see' my experience of you."[98]

I know something you don't know, and you know something I don't know. The knowledge I am talking about here is part of a person's life experience, and the knowledge the person is trying to express is linked to his life experience. When I say "knowledge" I do not mean the words, thoughts, ideas—I use this word to express the meaning it expresses. The same word, the same concept, has a completely different meaning for me and for you. In the beginning there is my meaning and your meaning. In the process of therapy we form our meaning, and it includes my meaning and your meaning— we both are involved in its construction. We are building something together. You are ahead of me, I follow you, expressing my readiness and being present to you at this moment. And this allows me to be not only "here and now," but also to be in the future, before it arrives. It is what the American psychologist Clark Moustakas, one of the founders of the Association for Humanistic Psychology, called *anticipatory caring*; Heidegger called *being towards*; and the French psychoanalyst André Green called *heralding anticipation*. Leo Tolstoy in his dialogue between Levin and Kitty creates a powerful image of such "anticipatory" relationships:

> *'I've long wanted to ask you one thing.'*
> *He looked straight into her caressing, though frightened eyes.*
> *'Please, ask it.'*
> *'Here,' he said; and he wrote the initial letters, w, y, t, m, i, c, n, b, d, t, m, n, o, t. These letters meant, 'When you told me it could never be, did that mean never, or then?' There seemed no likelihood that she could make out this complicated sentence; but he looked at her as though his life*

---

[98] Laing, R.D., *The Politics of Experience,* Routledge & Kegan Paul, 1967

depended on her understanding the words. She glanced at him seriously, then leaned her puckered brow on her hands and began to read. Once or twice she stole a look at him, as though asking him, 'Is it what I think?'

'I understand,' she said, flushing a little.

'What is this word?' he said, pointing to the n that stood for never.

'It means NEVER,' she said; 'but that's not true!'

He quickly rubbed out what he had written, gave her the chalk, and stood up. She wrote, t, i, c, n, a, d.

Dolly was completely comforted in the depression caused by her conversation with Alexey Alexandrovitch when she caught sight of the two figures: Kitty with the chalk in her hand, with a shy and happy smile looking upwards at Levin, and his handsome figure bending over the table with glowing eyes fastened one minute on the table and the next on her. He was suddenly radiant: he had understood. It meant, 'Then I could not answer differently.'

He glanced at her questioningly, timidly.

'Only then?'

'Yes,' her smile answered.

'And n...and now?' he asked.

'Well, read this. I'll tell you what I should like—should like so much!' she wrote the initial letters, i, y, c, f, a, f, w, h. This meant, 'If you could forget and forgive what happened.'

He snatched the chalk with nervous, trembling fingers, and breaking it, wrote the initial letters of the following phrase, 'I have nothing to forget and to forgive; I have never ceased to love you.'

She glanced at him with a smile that did not waver.

'I understand,' she said in a whisper.[99]

---

[99] Tolstoy, L., *Anna Karenina,* http://www.planetpublish.com/wp-content/uploads/2011/11/Anna_Karenina_NT.pdf, **p. 868-869**

Therapeutic Presence

Fifty minutes have beat in that heart of yours.

Ten times has the river flowed before you.

Daniil Kharms

Usually, when people talk about dialogue they mean a conversation between two people. This understanding may be an inheritance of the Socratic dialogues in which one person asks questions and the other gives proper responses. One person is a student, the other is a teacher. Even if they from time to time switch roles, the essence doesn't change. The change would be purely cosmetic. But the word *dialogue* comes from the Latin *dia* and *logos*: "through meaning." The conversation of the two would have been *duo logos*. And true dialogue presupposes a turn to meaning. Such a dialogue can happen in a group as well. The best example is Dostoyevsky's polyphonic dialogue.[100] All of Dostoyevsky's novels are dialogical. No one in Dostoyevsky's work has the last word, every word has the right to be heard, expressed, accepted or rejected. His novels are filled with multitudes of independent and unmerged voices and consciences.[101] Even independent phrases can seem so contradictory as to be incompatible. For example: "An inexhaustible love for him lay

---

[100] Bakhtin, M., *The Problems of Dostoyevsky's Poetics*, University of Minnesota Press, 1984
[101] Ibid.

concealed in her heart in the midst of continual hatred, jealousy, and contempt."[102]

"The possibility of simultaneous coexistence, the possibility of being side by side or one against the other, is for Dostoyevsky almost a criterion for distinguishing the essential from the nonessential. Only such things as can conceivably be linked together at a single point in time are essential and are incorporated into Dostoyevsky's world; such things can be carried over into eternity, for in eternity, according to Dostoyevsky, all is simultaneous, everything coexists."[103] Here one discovers an important principle of supratemporal functioning of conscience. "[I]f we inspect consciousness we find no past, present, future, but a unity embracing complexity. Everything is in consciousness, and everything in consciousness is and is together. There is in it a sensuous and a nonsensuous. We may call the sensuous--what we are seeing, hearing, touching--the 'present' while in the nonsensuous the vast image-world of memory is being labeled 'the past' and another realm of belief, intuition, and uncertainty 'the future'; yet sensation, memory, foresight, all are in consciousness together."[104]

The word *presence*, just like the German *anwesen* and the Russian *prisutstviye*, is a literal translation of the Latin *praesentia*, which means "being present." Heidegger understands *anwesen* as an act of presence, a protrusion of essence, an emergence from a hidden, secret state.[105] In Old German *anwesen* means a place for living, for inhabiting, a small estate, a plot of land, a village, a place where people live or exist. In Old Russian, *prisutstviye* is a government institution. Presence is connected to space, to a place of being, a place of search and wandering. While wandering, it is easy to get lost. A hero of Hassidic

---

[102] Dostoyevsky, F., trans. by Garnett, C., *The Possessed*

[103] Bakhtin, M., *The Problems of Dostoyevsky's Poetics*, University of Minnesota Press, 1984, p. 29

[104] Whorf, B.L., "The Relation to Habitual Thought and Behavior to Language", reprinted from *Language, culture, and personality, essays in memory of Edward Sapir,* Menasha, Wis.: Sapir Memorial Publication Fund, 1941, pp. 75-93,

[105] Carman, T., "Heidegger's concept of presence," *Inquiry: An Interdisciplinary Journal of Philosophy*, Vol. 38, issue 4, 1995, pp. 431-453

legends venerated by Buber[106] says that God's main question to man is "Where are you?" "Where are you, Adam?" is not merely a question, it is a question directed *at the very heart of things*: where are you in your life? And yet space appears to us tamer than time: we constantly run into people who carry watches but very rarely into people who carry compasses, as George Perec cleverly points out.[107]

Still, it has been noted a long time ago that the biggest tragedy for a person is precisely not knowing his or her place in life. And at the same time, that is the question that attracts people the most. Therapists talk about being "here and now" as a kind of real time-place, but they often forget that this time-place can only exist in a specific context. The space in which we exist is not an indifferent space, it is strung with invisible threads that connect us to various *incidents*. These events literally *co-incide* with us. It makes no sense to talk about "this moment in time" as if it is something that exists on its own. On its own, "I am walking down the street" or "I am sitting on a chair" makes no sense. Or, rather, it only makes sense in the context of where I am walking from, where I am walking to, what this space means to me, from which place within myself I see and experience this. And what is this moment in time in *my life*. Not the familiar five-minute-long stretch of linear time that is measured by the hands of a clock, but the difference in experience felt subjectively in time—the difference a child knows well when she asks, "Will these be five minutes at a Christmas party or five minutes in a doctor's office?" In order to pose the question this way, one has to look at the world in a special manner, to see in it not some self-sufficient details but to see also the context, to see what you see as an element of a broader figure or rule. One way or another, a person possesses a temporal direction, an orientation toward the future, a person becomes disoriented if this vector is lost.[108]

---

[106] Buber, M., *The Way of Man*

[107] Perec, G., *Species of Spaces and Other Pieces*, Penguin Classics, 2008, p. 75

[108] In some traditional cultures the understanding of the direction of time is different from the Western understanding of it. For example, according to one of the classifications of the Fulani, a nomadic people, or, rather, individual groups that live across West Africa, the world is divided into three temporal areas: "tomorrow," which is populated by ancestors; "today," where people

Therapeutic presence can be described, using Bakhtin's expression, as a therapist's "relations of tense omnipresence"[109] toward all the moments of the client's being—an omnipresence that is spatial, temporal, moral and contextual, which allows the client to emerge at a session wholly, as an integral being. At such moments, the boundaries of a session seem to loosen and are capable of including all the fullness of the client's life in his or her relationships with others and with the world, in which the mode of being that is familiar to the client appears as one of unfolding possibilities. At such moments the boundaries of time loosen and any life event becomes accessible for exploration and for establishing new relationships. *Omnipresence* presupposes not a horizontality or linearity of time, but a different understanding of time, an understanding that allows the potential of access to any moment. Because "[j]ust as a man still is what he always was, so he already is what he will become."[110]

One can, therefore, consider therapeutic presence as a complex professional skill. Even more than a skill, it is a way of co-existing in which the boundaries of the fabric of life is erased and the other person becomes as if *separated out* of the world; he or she becomes the only person in this world who at the same time emerges in the full multifariousness of his or her relationships and the singularity of his or her life journey, which is also interwoven with the life journeys of other people. A person is present *exactly at this very moment of his or her life* with all the emotions and feelings of this very moment of his or her life. Simultaneously, his or her life transpires a multibraided and one-of-a-kind stream interwoven with the many events and relationships of the past and the present, which at the same time are as if kept at a distance

---

live; and "yesterday," the world the person inhabited in the womb. Curiously, according to the Fulani the world of ancestors does not precede the world of today but exists in the future, ahead. (Zubko G.V., *Misteria ful'be//Amadu Hampate Ba, Kaidara*, Belovodye, 2008, p. 161)

[109] Bakhtin, M., *Avtor i geroi. K filosofskim osnovam gumanitarnykh nauk*, Azbuka, 2000, p. 41

[110] Jung, C., Jacobi, J., *Psychological Reflections: An Anthology of Jung's Writings 1905-1961*, Routledge, 1998, p. 306

for a moment, allowing the person to emerge from this stream and to become revealed to his or her potential.

In the image of a multibraided stream, there is depth, dynamism, fluidity. Heidegger understood presence as *presencing*, a process, a lasting emergence of essence, a coming out of secrecy, of hiddenness. If we rely on such understanding, we can talk about three aspects that are typical for presence: about the active nature of the process of being present; about its temporal endurance; and about the fact that, as a result of presence, we discover something previously unknown. Therefore, one can see, in the phenomenon of presence, a unique kind of cognition. It is unique because in it, the future comes alive.

The Time and Space of a Therapy Session

Time present and time past

Are both perhaps present in time future

And time future contained in time past.

If all time is eternally present

All time is unredeemable.

T. S. Eliot

"We all come from our childhood." This phrase is so banal that at first you have no desire to argue with it, you slip past it, you don't think about it. But the idea behind this phrase emerges from the blank spaces that await filling in. This thought is old, it has an ancient history. It comes from the tendency to look at childhood as something separate, isolated, as a space one can come out of. Boris Pasternak noted this once: "[Greece] understood how to meditate on childhood which is as sealed up and independent as an initial integrated kernel...In her opinion, some portion of risk and tragedy must be gathered sufficiently early in a handful which can be gazed upon and understood in a flash. Certain sections of the edifice...must be laid once and for all from the very outset in the interests of its future proportions."[111] The perception of a lifetime as linear—the perception typical for Western culture— stems from this concept of childhood as confined and isolated. First childhood, then youth. Then young adulthood. The childhood stays

---

[111] Pasternak, B., *Safe Conduct*, New Directions, 2009, pp. 24-25

somewhere behind. From here comes the perception of adulthood as some kind of terminal destination, as if time stops here. After adulthood there are only old age and death.

The French psychoanalyst André Green found in his studies of Freud's work 18 passages in which Freud refers to time. That is a lot. Freud considers important the concept of bi-directionality of the psychic processes—forward, toward the future, and backward, toward the past—because there are instances in which this movement is parallel. In a 2005 lecture,[112] Green noted that Freud had singled out thin concentric layers of memory, which he likened to an archive or a library. At the same time, Freud spoke of the presence of radial routes, which traveled through the strata of memory and the connecting elements that belonged to different strata. Besides, he compared the dualistic process of psychic functions to the behavior of a chess knight. The knight moves by jumping over pieces. Green finds the idea of a dualistic process that connects the radial and concentric routes original, novel at the time and not employed today.

Yet, a decade and a half before Green's lecture, in discussing the subject of non-linearity in psychic functions, American psychologists John Firman and Ann Gila used the metaphor of tree rings: each previous ring is surrounded by the next, but at the same time it does not disappear nor dissolve in the future or preceding rings, but remains present in the life of the whole tree at every given moment. They presented this idea at a psychosynthesis conference in Concord, Massachusetts, in 1994. Firman said that he had heard of this idea in Italy from Assagioli in 1973. Based on Assagioli's thoughts, Firman and Gila created a concentric model of personal development, in which each period or moment in life is included in the next and can make itself known at any moment. This way, time is permeated by the unity of life events.

---

[112] André Green. "Lectures. Freud's concept of temporality: Differences with current ideas." *The International Journal of Psychoanalysis*, 2008, vol. 89, issue 5, pp. 1029–1039

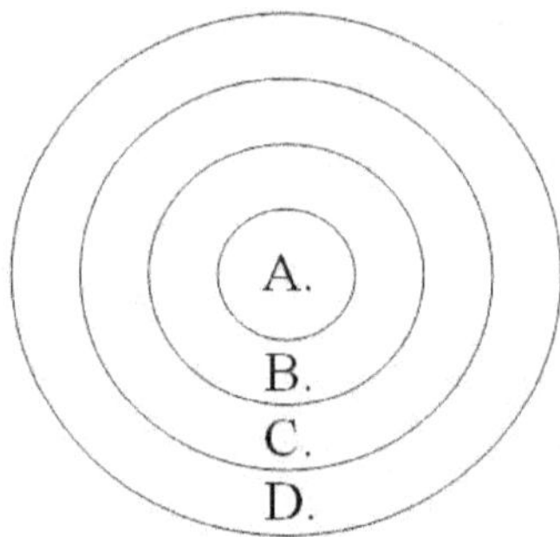

A. Infant
B. Child
C. Adolescent
D. Adult

Illustration III: Firman and Gila model of personal development[113]

If we transcend the formally-contextual framework of a session, we can see a cyclicality of a developing dialogue that is typical for the session, a dialogue that includes a client and a therapist. This process of a cyclical dialogue also includes the process of an internal dialogue. From the linear-monological point of view, the internal dialogue of a client may appear multidirectional and contradictory. However, if we are to consider the multifaceted and non-linear nature of the ongoing process, we will be able to see how various equal spacial-temporal layers of spiritual life coexist within a single flow. It is as if the boundaries between the past, present, and future are erased, and everything seems to be happening as if in the same moment, in the same ongoing process. The past remains in the past until we touch it—at which point it comes alive, becomes pliable, the perception of it is transformed and the events of the past obtain a new place in our conscience. The subconscious elements that emerge spontaneously become objectified and it becomes possible to establish a conscious connection to them. Aspects that once seemed contradictory lose their rigidity and staleness, obtain fluidity and are filled with new energy.

This creates conditions that allow a client to see what he or she could not see until then, to hear what until then had been mute. It is not necessary that what emerges is something the client does not know about herself or himself, but it is possible that it is something the client

---

[113] Firman, J., Gila, A., *A Psychotherapy of Love. Psychosynthesis in Practice.* SUNY Press, 2010, p. 32

has not reflected upon before, something he or she has not thought about. The client may see signs that point to the difference between the image of himself or herself that he or she is used to, and his or her true self; the client may discover the potential for change and movement toward him or herself.

Life's journey travels through time because of incongruences and movement of its strata, because of the connection and continuity of the coalescences of life events that transcend the boundaries of the "presentness" of some "present moment" that took place at one point and that continues to limit them.

You must have heard five- or six-year-old children at play use a formula that describes the future using past tense, "Let's play that I was a doctor and you were the patient," or "Let's play that I was a teacher and you were a student." Such past tense is more reminiscent of a future tense turned inside out. Adults, too, prefer to ignore the future as the future and to experience it in terms of the past or the present. They explain this rationally by saying that because the future has not yet arrived, they simply cannot know it and have no access to it. There is a famous metaphor that describes a person as a rower on a boat. His gaze is on the stern, and he sees only the past—that is, that from which he has sailed away. His back is turned to what lies ahead, to the future, he cannot see it and has no way to access it; and in his hands are the oars—the present in which he can act at will. The rower nonetheless has decided for some reason to sail toward whatever he is sailing to, from wherever he is sailing from, and because of this something happens in his soul, which is to say, there exists certain context. It is hard to imagine that he is sailing without having any idea where he is planning to arrive. Without having any *intentions* in this regard. Without *anticipating*, we couldn't even simply cross a road.

The fact that we ostensibly do not know the future does not mean that we have no access to it (even if we call it a possible future). Our experience shows that we don't even know our present as well as we sometimes believe—at least, the meaning of facts changes for us as time passes. Sometimes this meaning changes radically. So we may just as well claim that we live in a possible present. Regardless of the terms, grammatical tenses, and moods the future uses to define itself, it is important to help a person see and recognize this stratum so that life can obtain its characteristic temporal dimension and become flexible and fluid, and this can be a therapeutic task. John Kafka writes that clients are impelled by the need to expand the reality in which they live and function, the need to transcend accepted limitations. The past can be experienced as something dead, stale, something that has slipped out of life. It can be softened and brought to life once it is placed in a new context of a therapeutic situation, in which, after repeated therapeutic contact and under new circumstances, it emerges in the current temporal dimension and therefore becomes meaningful.[114] Through the softening in the relationship with the therapist during a session, the petrified past comes back to life, regains fluidity and empties out into the present. Beyond the present moment, the meaning that obtained its fluidity in the river of time arrives at a new context of new facts and there manifests itself differently.

We are surrounded by contexts of meanings, emerged in them, meanings flow through us, between us. Meanings can exist potentially, in hidden form, and emerge in favorable new contexts that are formed within a therapeutic space. Change stems from here. In order to experience change we must enter into a relationship with a certain facet of emotion that is a harbinger of change, we must feel the fluidity of the process. And we can learn to enter the relationship with the flow of experience, a natural process that seems to be hidden; we can be aware of the meanings that are as-yet implied, not yet obvious, as we broaden the context of our seeing. Each experience of an event essentially contains the potential for future development—one can say it is pregnant with the possibility of change. This presupposes a therapeutic openness to the unknown, to the mystery, to what has not yet emerged.

Turning to the future is reflected in the concept of acceptance as an *affirmation of the potentiality of the Other*. For Martin Buber *affirmation* goes farther than acceptance because acceptance refers first and foremost to what is right now, whereas affirmation refers to the acceptance of

---

[114] Kafka, J., *Multiple Realities in Clinical Practice*, Yale University Press, 1989

the entire potential, to what this particular person has a calling to become ("being a man to become," says Buber). By approaching the other in this way, not only do I accept him or her the way he/she is, but also the way he/she has the potential to become. And in this way I affirm this potential for him/her and for myself. Somehow this begins to be shared between us. Now I and this person can both relate to it in some way and influence it. Both of us can help this potential to become real, to care for it. I think we know well that such potential can take place between, for example, a loving husband and wife, or between a parent and a child. When one says to the other, "I accept you the way you are," it does not mean that such acceptance limits her in her possible changes. It is not at all the same as saying, "I don't want you to change." On the contrary, in this case it means: "I accept you the way you are intended to become, the way you can become. And it does not necessarily have to be expressed in words. Rather, the entire relationship itself can express it.[115]

There exists this clever definition of space and time: Space is what makes objects different from one another, and time is what makes objects different from themselves. Only with the passage of time is it possible to perceive the changes within. Time is what allows us to perceive change inside ourselves—and not merely to perceive change but also to enter into a relationship with this change. The relationship between people is the state of being inside time.

All of us know from experience that some moments can stretch almost eternally, while certain months or even years can contract and even vanish without leaving a visible trace. Time can slow down, stretch, stop, fly by unnoticed. Time can be full, lost, wasted. It may be difficult to comprehend the following quote from Merab Mamardashvili (though it reads like poetry) but it does carry a special meaning for psychotherapists:

> *Only the future preserves the past,*
> *and only the preserved past*
> *allows for change (and not for a repeat).*

---

[115] Buber, M., *Martin Buber on Psychology and Psychotherapy: Essays, Letters, and Dialogues*, Syracuse University Press, 1999, p. 267.

> *If something did not come into existence yesterday*
> *there cannot be any existence today.*
> *And if we do not change today*
> *then nothing will be preserved.*[116]

Where there is no time there is no flexibility, no fluidity, there is no change. Where there is no change there is no time, we only repeat ourselves, we do not change, we become stuck. Therapeutic relationships do not tolerate staleness. They always demand renewal.

The healing strength of the present is in its ability to be aware. Now one can conceive of existence. Now one can relate to it. Now the creative act of change is possible. And even before, in the very rejection of unknowing, in the stubbornness of effort in the face of challenge, in the openness to encounter, one can see the act of will toward change: it is through the awareness of the present that the future is born.

---

[116] Mamardashvili, M., *Strela poznanija, Nabrosok istoricheskoy gnosseologii*, Jaziki russkoy kulturi, 1996, p. 210-211

Psychotherapy in Social Context

(In Lieu of an Afterword)

In 2014, immediately after this book was published in Russian, events occurred that shook the world: in March, Russia essentially annexed Crimea, and war began in Eastern Ukraine. This happened suddenly, although it was possible to predict the course of the military conflict with Ukraine by how Russian newscasts gradually regressed into passionate hatred, anger and rage toward the social changes that were taking place in Ukraine. The war continues as I write. In fact, I am writing because the war continues. It is because of the war that I decided to add another chapter to my book.

Sometimes it happens that when you are engrossed in something, when you are looking for a way out of a complicated situation, an answer can come from the least expected direction. I often find answers in texts. Back in March 2014, I was able to attend a performance of Arvo Pärt's "Adam's Lament." In the playbill that members of the audience found placed on their seats when they entered the theater, the composer responded to the question of whether the title of the composition was referring to a specific event:

Usually I don't comment on my music. But, you're right, this piece contains a certain message. About what was the beginning of everything and what everything has come to. We are Adam's heirs. Great was his sorrow when he saw his son killed by his own brother Cain. And he thought, as the Bible puts it, that people will come of me and will fill all the Earth. And they will form great nations. And they will hate and kill each other. And that's what happened.

I listened to the music and thought: here we are, alive, but Cain's deed is also alive with us, and we have to be with it somehow. I thought that this was the very gist of the human condition: evil is always within our field of vision, and we are always within its reach. And all of our circumstances (remember Ortega y Gasset's "I am I and my circumstances") constitute our *I*.

After the concert I took a walk and thought, so how do I, how do we, *be with it?* We the professionals, the psychotherapists—since this is our *I*, too.

I once read the words of an anonymous German author, who said a week before the beginning of World War II: "This is it. Had I really been a writer I would have been able to prevent the war." One could say that the author at the very least exaggerated his role as a writer. But there is another way to interpret this quote: it is not surprising that a person who works with words more than anyone else hopes that words have influence. War is a collision of interests. In order to make people risk their lives in the name of interests, one has to make an effort to transform their perception of reality. Including through words. And I thought, we, too, work through words. And so, we, too, have our role and our share of responsibility.[117]

Of course, time has passed since that anonymous author wrote those words, new technologies have appeared, and contemporary

---

[117] Remember Buber: "A dog has looked at you, you answer for its glance, a child has clutched your hand, you answer for its touch, a host of men moves about you, you answer for their need." (Buber, M., *Between Man and Man*, Routledge, 2002, p. 20). In order to understand this thought we have to recall what Buber means when he talks about responsibility: "The idea of responsibility is to be brought back from the province of specialized ethics, of an 'ought' that swings free in the air, into that of lived life. Genuine responsibility exists only where there is real responding. Responding to what? To what happens to one, to what is to be seen and heard and felt. Each concrete hour allotted to the person, with its content drawn from the world and from destiny, is speech for the man who is attentive. Attentive, for no more than that is needed in order to make a beginning with the reading of the signs that are given to you. (Ibid, pp. 18-19)

media has made possible projects that construct worlds (including with words) in which the real and the false, truth and lies, are so intertwined that it becomes impossible to distinguish one from another. Hanna Arendt called this defactualization. What *seems* displaces what *is*, the reality of events is displaced by their alleged versions. These versions are mutually contradictory and, as such, leave the recipient stunned into a kind of a trance.

The principle of reality is replaced by the principle of a lie, and this leads to the metamorphosis of public consciousness, causes passivity, inertia.

How can we counter it?

In 2007, two years after the devastation of the hurricane Katrina, my American friend Diana Rossman wrote in a letter:

> *With all due respect to those still suffering from the hurricane here in New Orleans, as well as those suffering the effect of mass disasters (natural and unnatural) throughout the world, I find myself living with the analogy/parallel experience that each of us is living in a time of impending disaster, disaster, and the aftermath of disaster, all at the same time, all the time. Whether the hurricane is within or without, whether it is coming or predicted to come, my challenges and my practice seem to be cultivating stillness, presence of mind (staying awake), presence of heart (staying fateful) and presence of will (staying engaged). I struggle.*

We all struggle; we all do the best we can.

I saw a similar thought in the stunning brevity and precision of the words by the Russian writer Mikhail Prishvin: "Clarity of the soul, its peace. Truth of the lips and the actions. Courage."[118] He wrote these words in his diary in the terrible year of 1937, the year the Soviet Union exterminated millions of its own people.

How to preserve presence, balance, how to remain involved? How to obtain the clarity of the soul and its peace? How to observe the truth of actions and courage? How to counter apocalyptic consciousness, when the mind refuses to process the changes that take place in the

---

[118] Prishvin, M.M., *Dnevniki 1937. Chast'* II. http://www.fedy-diary.ru/?page_id=5430

world, and it seems that everything around is collapsing? I ask myself these questions as well, and I think many people today ask themselves these questions.

I think these are questions of a professional position. Of qualities that we, as specialists, must develop or cultivate within ourselves.

I often hear that we are living at the time of enormous change. When people recognize their own time as a time of change it typically means that the conventional order that once seemed inviolable is dramatically collapsing. But is change, including dramatic change, not a part of human circumstances in general? Looking back at the last two decades, it is hard to ignore the constant accompaniment of wars. Different wars. In Chechnya, in Afghanistan, in Iraq, in the Balkans, in Rwanda, in the Middle East, in Syria, in Ukraine… When these events happen to someone else, when they do not concern us directly, when we look at them from afar, we prefer to search for rational explanations for their awfulness. (As if such explanations exist!) Searching for rational explanations comforts us, and as a rule we do find rational explanations, and we accept the reality as something inevitable and acquiesce to it, comply with it. And in this way, in the clever words of the French philosopher André Glucksmann, for a small intellectual price we obtain a certificate of angelic impartiality.

Our task, however, is not to calm down but, in allowing ourselves to see the essence of what is happening, to recognize its complexity. Our task is not to simplify this complexity but rather, stirred by it, to establish a dialogue with the different ideas that are in conflict with one another. To find—first and foremost in ourselves—the space, the locus, from which we can undertake the internal effort to allow all the participants of the conflict to talk equally, to create an opportunity for dialogue. Then we can project such a locus externally.

In the beginning of this book, I describe the conference called "War and Trauma," which Harmony organized in 2000, at the peak of the Second Chechen War. The conference brought together, for the first time, representatives of human rights organizations, armed forces, school psychologists, public figures, journalists, doctors. At Harmony we saw it as our task to create space for dialogue. From the very start of the conference, the tension and the intolerance among the participants were extremely high. And yet, there were moments when the participants, who saw themselves as occupying opposite sides of the barricades, and who until then had never been able to listen and hear one another, were able to see the humanity of one another. At the very least, they saw the possibility of dialogue, and for them this was a huge discovery. And we, the organizers, were reassured that bringing together irreconcilable parties in one physical space can, by the very fact of co-presence, have an important impact on the transformation of conflict.

The tools for conflict resolution are also changing. Take a look, for example, at the evolution of which kinds of therapeutic approaches and directions were used in our country from this vantage point. In the Soviet times, these were typically manipulative techniques such as autogenic training, hypnosis, and other methods of inculcation and the so-called "rational psychotherapy." Until the 1970s, there existed no practical psychologists in the Soviet Union at all. There was no trade literature in practical psychology.

Naturally, after the Soviet Union collapsed, it became possible for domestic specialists to learn different therapeutic approaches and directions. New educational programs appeared, new institutes and training centers, and international exchange began. Remember Michel Foucault, who talked about *discontinuity* in culture—a phenomenon when, over the course of just a few years, a certain culture stops thinking the way it had thought theretofore and begins to think differently and about different things?[119] That's what it was like during perestroika. What I'm saying is that discontinuity is not bad, it means a culture, a society, shows signs of life. It's good. It means it's alive. And approaches will inevitably continue to change because the accents, the needs in a society will change. I want to focus on one such need in particular. *The post-Soviet psychotherapy specifically responded to the painful aspects of the process of change.* All sorts of previously hidden or suppressed conflicts came to life in the country, and this required the creation of

---

[119] Foucault, M., *The Order of Things: An Archaeology of the Human Sciences,* Pantheon Books, 1970

a system of emergency psychological help (over a short period of time hundreds of crisis intervention centers had sprung up—free hotline services, so one cannot explain their proliferation by any kind of economic imperative). A lot of psychotherapeutic work began with people suffering from PTSD: programs to help Afghan and Chechen war veterans, people who had worked at the sites of manmade catastrophes.

However, the main source of the problem lay not in the external consequences of the Soviet regime, but in its internal legacy: in the phenomenon of dehumanization that is typical for a totalitarian society, in the gradual loss of people's capacity to commiserate, be compassionate toward other living beings.

In truth, the seeming self-worth of psychotherapeutic approaches and methods is contextualized by culture. Salvatore D. Maddi at Harvard University once pointed out that the healing potential of any particular therapeutic approach depends on the dosage of its break with the dominant culture. The success of Freudian psychoanalysis in the early 20th century was related to the scandal it introduced to the puritanism of that time; this disconnect accelerated Freud's success. The success of nondirective therapy was stimulated by the one-dimensionality of the therapeutic style of the postwar era in North America. The idea that a split with the dominant culture results in a demand for therapy is very interesting. It is possible that the success of the proliferation of existential and humanistic approaches in Russia, which coincided with the collapse of the Soviet Union, can be explained by the reaction to the cruelty and rigidity of the Soviet system.

In 1968, the French psychologist Marc Richelle posed the question, "Why psychologists?" His question was a reaction to what he at the time called the sudden and "disquieting proliferation of a new species." His French colleague Didier Deleule offered a very radical explanation of this phenomenon: psychologists were proliferating because society at the time demanded an ideology of change, and psychologists provided such ideology. Psychologists offered an alternative solution to social conflicts, writes Deleule, by trying to change an individual while preserving a social order, or, at the very least, creating an illusion that if an individual changes, then the social order also may change.[120] One can take issue with Deluele's assertion. After all, changes in an individual, changes in a group, lead to broader changes in a society. Such a phenomenon is called parallelism.

Note when this dialogue took place: 1968. At the time, France was experiencing an enormous social crisis. At first glance, it seemed inexplicable. It originated with university students against a background of seeming wellbeing. France at the time was the largest economic power in Europe. The sudden student uprisings eventually caused a regime change, the resignation of the president, and vast social changes in French society. (One could compare it to the "color" revolutions of today.) It was precisely at that time that Marc Richelle wrote about what he called the sudden and "disquieting proliferation of a new species"—psychologists.

Today my country is also experiencing a "disquieting proliferation" of psychologists. In recent years, there has been a significant upswing in the popular interest in this profession. An example: a major psychological festival that took place in Moscow in April of 2011, called "A Human Planet." The festival lasted just a few days but thousands of people took part in it. People who attended it still recall with disbelief the enormous crowds of participants rushing to auditoriums in order to grab a seat at a workshop or a seminar. There has been an obvious increase in the number of people in Russia who want to be trained in the field of psychology. In 2014, many education centers received twice the number of applications from potential students than the year before. If one were to draw a parallel with 1960s France, one could see this as a testimony to the ripening of a need for change in our society. Similar processes take place in a society on a structural level, and, possibly, speak of the role of psychologists in the processes of social transformation.

In this context we can draw yet another parallel: between psychologists and educators. To support this comparison, I will turn

---

[120] Martin-Baro, I. *Writing for a Liberation Psychology*, First Harvard University Press paperback edition,1996, p. 37.

to the experience of the wonderful Brazilian educator Paulo Freire. According to his view, teaching literacy (Freire taught literacy to the underprivileged) means not merely teaching to read words, but also teaching to read the world. This requires switching on *critical thinking* (*conscientização*). People learn to "read their world" so they can act as subjects in the creation of a democratic society. Freire used the process of dialogue between a teacher and the students in which both sides learned, both sides questioned, both sides reflected and took part in creating new meaning.[121]

Freire believed that the goal of the education process was not in obtaining new knowledge about a subject, but in changing people's understanding of their existence and their internal position toward the world. The same is true for psychotherapy. In the process of therapy people obtain a deeper connection to their experience, it becomes harder to manipulate them, they become more independent. And I am not talking about the cult of individualism: I mean people's ability to relate to their internal world. Because of this ability, people become closer to themselves, to who they are.

In the summer of 2014, I ran across the 1983 article *The Structure of Empathy*,[122] and I would like to take the time to talk about it. It presents the result of the factor analysis of Hogan's Empathy Scale. The researchers identified four basic factors that constitute the scale: *Social Self-Confidence*, *Even Temperedness*, *Sensitivity* and *Nonconformity*.

Now let's take a look at what constitutes these "building blocks" of empathy, which statements turned out to be key for each of them:

Social Self-Confidence
I usually take an active part in the entertainment at parties.
I am a good mixer.
I have a natural talent for influencing people.
I think I am usually a leader in my group.

---

[121] Freire, P., *Pedagogy of the Oppressed*, Bloomsbury Academic, 2000
[122] Johnson, J., Cheek, J., Smither, R., "The Structure of Empathy", *Journal of Personality and Social Psychology*, 1983, Vol. 45, No. 6, pp. 1299-1312

I like to talk before groups of people.

The majority of the people who score high on the empathy scale agree with these and similar statements.

Even Temperedness

I am usually calm and not easily upset.

I am not usually angered.

The majority of the people who score high on the empathy scale agree with these statements.

I easily become impatient with people.

The majority of the people who score high on the empathy scale disagree with this statement.

But this is obvious. What is interesting is that the former two factors were less meaningful than the latter two. Which is to say, in the structure of empathy the critical factors are *sensitivity* and *nonconformism*.

Let's focus on them:

Sensitivity

I have at one time or another tried my hand at writing poetry.

I have seen some things so sad that I almost felt like crying.

The majority of the people who score high on the empathy scale agree with these statements.

What others think of me doesn't bother me.

I don't really care whether people like me or dislike me.

The majority of the people who score high on the empathy scale disagree with these statements.

Nonconformity

Disobedience to the government is never justified.

It bothers me when something unexpected interrupts my daily routine.

I like to have a place for everything and everything on its place.

It is the duty of a citizen to support his country, right or wrong.

The majority of the people who score high on the empathy scale disagree with these statements.

Let us pause here, because I see in this an expression of a very important professional condition. At the time, in 1983, when this research took place, the concepts of *metacognition* and *mentalization* (Fonagy) had not yet become popular. In essence, mentalization is the ability to see oneself from without and the Other from within. I think one must develop this ability not only on an individual but also on a cultural level. We must be continuously learning to see our cultural field from within and from without. So that we can "read the world." So that we can recognize and reflect context in which we exist with our clients.

The inability to "read the world" inevitably leads to distancing from life. The need for order, for maintaining traditions, and the inability to transcend the boundaries of traditions lead to the lifelessness of abstract schemes.

The development of the ability to "read the world" makes me think of Merab Mamardasvili's idea about learning to be "the spies of an unknown motherland."[123] "Radical doubt," says Mamardashvili, characterizes a "spy of an unknown motherland." Because ahead of us lies mystery. The unknown. That is why, in Marcel Proust's words, we have to have "antennae of disbelief, antennae of suspicion." We rebuild whole from scraps, from shreds. And so—let us doubt. And let us not be afraid of contradictions but invite them. Let us value chaos.

Our goal is to create a space in which people can change. We don't need to be afraid to go too far because the truth, as Proust says, is even farther. In the world of therapy, there exists only the truth of the moment, the truth of right now that serves the present. There is no room for objectivity. This truth appears and immediately disappears. It is subjective. In psychotherapy, truth is a process, not a thing. Here, truth cannot be discovered the way a chemical element can be discovered, or America. It cannot be hard as a rock, it is alive while there is blood flowing through its veins. When someone attempts to

---

[123] Mamardashvili, M., *Topologiya puti*, Lecture 6.

make it solid it first becomes dense, then painful, then fragile and sclerotic. Then such truth dies.

But there also exists a different kind of truth. For ages we have known about the natural impulse rooted in the human heart, the act of will that determines our ability to tell good from evil. Medieval Christian monks called it *synderesis*. Goethe, in *Faust*, spoke of an "ancient truth" that exists in each of us: "Hold tightly onto it, this ancient truth!" ("*Das alte Wahre, faß es an!*")

Everything depends on the ability to hold tightly onto the "ancient truth," on our ability to hold on and stand tall. Each of us possesses, and has always possessed, a certain internal compass that directs us, a compass to which it is important for us to develop access within ourselves. We have to "recalibrate" ourselves over and over. It depends on us, ourselves. It depends on whether we are trying to excel in becoming what we can become, what we are meant to become. But there are no guarantees. We ourselves have to undertake our own journey by making this effort again and again. We have to change ourselves, we have to take risks, because we can't learn by doing what someone else does, by copying someone else. But we cannot learn on our own, either. It requires a community.

There is a widespread belief that in order to perform deep self-work we need solitude, and such a journey is considered spiritual. Yet this is only one of the possible routes of such a journey. A very different spirituality consists of endeavoring to be fully alive, and in this way to generate a little bit more life around us. By some serendipity almost thirty years ago, a small group of searching friends, in what at the time was the Soviet Union, encountered their American colleagues who had set out toward them first, who, despite fears and prejudices, had performed an act of will and journeyed to a world about which they had known very little. And that improbable, "impossible" encounter gave birth to a long-lasting creative collaboration that impacted hundreds, thousands of people.

We live in a difficult time. But when has it been different? The situation in the world is very murky but now we know how it *can be*. Now we have an example, our own. And we know that so much of what *can be,* depends on us, ourselves. It depends on each of us. So in order to survive as humans we must take the way of humanity, we must live in the field of humanity.

Resonance, process, balance, acceptance, presence, perception of the inner beauty, space, time: all of these are the categories that reflect the multidimensionality of our experience of the field. This multidimensionality is precisely what determines their value for a therapist, which is why I believe that it is necessary to turn to them, to study them. Not that the field is somewhere "out there" and the therapist is here. The therapist is a part of this field, and he or she must recognize the mechanisms of his or her influence on the intensity of the field, to manage the ability to hold its intensity.

Acknowledgments

I would like to thank my old friend Gary Whited, a psychotherapist and a poet, for the title of this book. A couple of years ago, while I was writing it, Gary and I met in Boston and, as usually happens during our meetings, we talked about philosophy, poetry, and psychotherapy. At one point Gary told me about his philosophy teacher, Henry Bugbee, and said that Bugbee was once referred to as a "lyrical philosopher," although he would not have called himself by that name.

The very notion of lyrical philosophy touched me and seemed to reflect with great precision the gist of what I wanted to write about psychotherapy. Not only did this expression give a title for the Russian version of my book (in Russian it is called *A Lyrical Philosophy of Psychotherapy*.) but defined the general direction of my thinking. For me lyrical philosophy is the kind of philosophy that reaches not merely one's mind but also one's heart: it is a philosophy with human eyes. It cannot remain detached; it engages in the world of relationships. This way, thinking is directed not at obtaining new knowledge about a subject, but rather, at changing our understanding of being and our internal perspective in relationship to the world. It is tangible. That is its goal and purpose. And this is where psychotherapy, lyricism, and philosophy intersect. I wrote a book based on these suppositions. I tried to describe the therapeutic process from within. For all of it I'm grateful to Henry Bugbee and to Gary who passed Henry's gift on to me.

I am grateful to my closest friends, first and foremost, to Mark Pevzner, one of Harmony's co-founders, and to Thomas Yeomans, Mark's and my friend, mentor and supporter, who helped us realize our dream to create the International School for Psychotherapy, Counseling and Group Leadership in St. Petersburg. For many years, I have had the support of my friends Mark Horowitz and David Elliott.

My friendship with them has been my lodestar during the most difficult of times. Regardless of what went on in my life I always knew that I could rely on you. Thank you, Mark and David.

I also very much would like to express my gratitude to many people I have encountered along the way. Some of them I mentioned in the book. In some cases, only by name. But trust me: my heart is full of sincere gratitude for the support and the priceless experience I have acquired with the help from all of them. Claire Boskin, Prilly Sanville, Anne Yeomans, Lenore Lefer, Michael Gigante, Molly Brown, Philip Brooks, Abby Seixas, Steven Schatz, Dory Fliegel from the United States; Nils Grendstad from Norway; Marcel Rheault and André Paré from Canada—you were invaluable guides in the beginning of my journey. Thank you.

I am thankful to Steve Olweean and Maryanne Olsen, with whom we co-coordinated international conferences for helping professionals for many years in the 1990's. I learned a great deal from my experience in this collaboration.

Over the years we have received crucial supplemental financial resources from friends and colleagues in the United States. It is impossible to overestimate the effect of this support from Wendy and Jerielle and from Barbara and Jacques. Thank you, dear friends.

I particularly want to thank my American friends for making it possible to translate this book and publish it in English. A special thank you to Mark Horowitz, who initiated this process and went through the trouble of raising funds for the translation and publication of this book and helped to put this book together in general. Without Mark's generosity this English publication would not have been possible.

Naturally, I am grateful to my clients. I also am grateful to my colleagues from the Harmony Institute for Psychotherapy and Counseling. All of them, directly or indirectly, have influenced my professional outlook. I am especially thankful to Viktor Kagan, who read my manuscript and responded with a series of valuable comments.

My eldest daughter Anna Badkhen found the time to translate the book into English. I am certain that her translation and edits have changed the book for the better. Thank you so much, Anya.

My deepest gratitude is to my wife, Marina Badkhen, for her support, inspiration and indispensable help in creating and editing this book.

About the Author

Alexander Badkhen is one of the founders of the Institute for Psychotherapy and Counseling HARMONY, director of the International School for Psychotherapy, Counseling and Group Leadership (St. Petersburg, Russia). He is an honorable member of professional guild of Psychotherapy and Training (St. Petersburg). Psychiatrist, psychotherapist, supervisor. He may be reached at alexanderbadkhen@gmail.com